Perfect D

LAKE GARDA

Contents

 TOP 10 4

That Lake Garda Feeling 6

For chapters: See inside front cover

Not to be missed!

Our TOP 10 hits – from the absolute No. 1 to No. 10 – help you plan your tour of the most important sights.

★ SIRMIONE ➤ 50

Beautifully located on the south of the lake, Sirmione boasts one of the best preserved moated fortresses in Europe.

★ MALCESINE & MONTE BALDO ➤ 78

The 13th-century Castello Scaligero (left) is one of the best-known landmarks on Lake Garda; **Monte Baldo** a place to escape the heat of summer down on the water.

★ GARDA ➤ 83

With its wonderful lakeside promenade (Lungolago), Punta di San Vigilio around the corner and Isola del Garda a few minutes away by boat, the variety of attractions Lake Garda has to offer can all be enjoyed from just one place.

★ SALÒ ➤ 55

Reminders of the town's eventful history can be seen all down Lungolago, one of the most elegant promenades on the lake with a sophisticated atmosphere to match.

★ RIVA DEL GARDA ➤ 85

This little town became the haunt of poets, writers and philosophers at the turn of the 20th century. Its *grandezza* and beautiful architecture can still be seen today.

★ PIAZZA BRA & ARENA DI VERONA ➤ 102

Who wouldn't want to sit on Verona's world-famous square, gazing at the Roman amphitheatre and dream of being Romeo or Juliet?

★ PIAZZA DEI SIGNORI ➤ 108

Shakespeare may be better known but the memorial in the centre of Verona honours another great writer, the poet Dante Alighieri who wrote his masterpiece, the *Divine Comedy*, in this city.

★ PIAZZA DELLE ERBE ➤ 111

Verona's 'belly' – its market – provides a stage for everyday life set against a magnificent backdrop of *palazzi* from various eras and the Torre dei Lamberti.

★ BERGAMO ➤ 128

The *Città Alta* (Old Town) with the Piazza Vecchia is one of the most beautiful in northern Italy. Simply taking the *funicolare* from the lower town is an experience in itself.

★ LAGO D'ISEO ➤ 133

Framed by wooded slopes in the southern foothills of the Alps, Lago d'Iseo has the longest lake island in Central Europe – Monte Isola – with a scattering of idyllic villages, olive groves, cherry and chestnut trees.

THAT
LAKE GARDA

Discover what makes Lake Garda as appealing as it is and experience its unique flair. Just as the locals do.

THE FIRST ESPRESSO AFTER LEAVING THE *AUTOSTRADA*

Stop at the car park after the first hairpin bend coming from Nago heading for Torbole and enjoy your first cup of coffee, your first *aperol* or your first ice cream (at the bar on the other side of the road). The view to the south is breathtaking.

RACING THROUGH TUNNELS LIKE JAMES BOND

The Gardesana Occidentale that runs down the western side of the lake from Campione to Riva passes through at least a dozen tunnels which even inspired 007's motive scouts. Bond & Co. spent two weeks filming for *Quantum of Solace* on Lake Garda. That may only have resulted in a brief moment in the final film – but what a couple of minutes!

TRIP ON A PADDLE STEAMER

A trip across the lake on the 'Zanardelli' or the 'Italia' – two paddle steamers built in 1903 and 1908 respectively – is a must. The 'Zanardelli' operates in the north; the 'Italia' in the south. The locals love being out on the lake too, albeit generally in their own

On your marks: surfers in Torbole never have to wait long for the right wind to blow

FEELING

sailing boats. Alternatively you can hire a little motorboat with 40hp even if you don't have a driving licence.

TORBOLE AT HALF-PAST-SIX

When the first rays of sunlight peak over Monte Baldo the lake is already full of brightly coloured sails. When the wind is right, the windsurfing cracks are out on the water by this time, speeding along or showing off their tricks. Distance fans race back and forth along a 2km (1¼mi) stretch between Torbole and Riva as if on a conveyor belt. Time and again. A wonderful spectacle to watch.

That Lake Garda Feeling

A VIEW OF THE LAKE AND PASTA AT HALF-PAST-SEVEN

In the evening, when the colour of the lake changes from a brilliant silver to a soft gold in the light of the setting sun, sit back and enjoy an *aperol* or a 'Hugo' before your evening meal on the Gardesana Orientale at least once during your stay and watch the sun go down – either on a pontoon in Torri del Benaco, a balcony in the 'Belvedere' in Marniga di Brenzone or right on the water with a view of the castle in Malcesine on the Lido di Paina.

SUNDAY EVENING ON THE BEACH

Lots of Italian families head for the lakeside in July and August even although it is often said that it is firmly in the hands of the Germans – which, considering the number of tourists who flood to the lake every year, is hardly surprising. However, when the Italians descend the situation changes noticeably. Tables, chairs and sun umbrellas appear early in the morning and airbeds are pumped up. After a long, hot day, family get-togethers start at around half past seven in the evening with barbecues, *vino* and a huge variety of *antipasti*. And some of the fathers may have had a successful day's fishing. You may even be invited to a glass of something by your neighbours.

A DAY IN A DESERTED VILLAGE

A 30-minute walk along a a donkey track from Marniga di Brenzone will bring you to Campo. An artist has set up his easel, sheep are grazing nearby, a donkey is standing motionless in the blazing sun. Campo dates from the 11th century and is a quiet, solitary place albeit run down now. Hardly anyone lives here anymore as most people have moved away: no roads, no future – but a wonderful atmosphere.

A NIGHT IN THE LIMONAIA

The view of the bulbous lower end of the lake is simply stunning and the edge of the infinity pool merges optically with the water on Lake Garda 300m (985ft) below. You may be able to find a more exclusive place to stay in Lago, but nowhere is a beautiful as in "Lefay" – the holiday resort above Gargnano (► 69) that will give you that perfect 'lago' feeling.

Lefay Resort: a little bit of luxury never did any harm

The Magazine

The **MOUNTAINS,** the **RIVER** and the **LAKES**

Sandwiched between the Alps to the north and the Apennines in the south is the Lombardy Plain. This low-lying, fertile region is bisected by the River Po. The river rises below Monte Viso – near Italy's western border with France – in Piedmont, named after its location at the 'foot of the mountains'. The river then flows eastwards, prevented from turning north or south by the mountain massifs and, on its way, it collects the water that flows out of the great lakes which define the geography of northern Italy.

During the Pleistocene Ice Age, a period of about 1.5 million years, the movement of huge glaciers from the Alps followed the line of least resistance between ridges of harder rock. As they advanced the glaciers gouged out the valleys and ground the loose rock to a paste which was deposited as a moraine at the sides and head of the glacier. When the ice finally retreated, freshwater lakes, dammed by the moraine, formed in the extra deep valleys.

While other lakes in northern Italy are long and thin and confined to their valleys, Lake Garda owes its axe shape to the Piedmont glacier that formed it, so-called because once it moved away from the foot of the mountains the ice spread out sideways as well as flowing forwards, forming a wide 'foot'.

Fertile Shores

Lake Garda's fertile shores and abundance of freshwater fish attracted human settlers from the earliest times. The wide band of rich soil around the edge of the lake was formed by the magnesium-rich limestone brought down as a glacial moraine from the Brenta Dolomites to the north. On the northern shore the strip of fertile moraine is much narrower. In places on the western shore the high ridge descends directly into the lake. On this shore agriculture was more difficult, although more concentrated crops flourished – olives and vines on the eastern side, lemons on the west.

Hiking from the Pregasina tunnel towards Riva, Lake Garda can be seen at its very best.

Today the vines are still there, growing grapes for Bardolino wines. Olive trees still flourish here too, giving the eastern shore its name – the Olive Riviera – although cultivation is now less than it was. Only a few *limonaie* growing lemon trees are to be found now on the western 'Lemon coast'.

LAKE GARDA'S STATISTICS

- Lake Garda covers an area of 370km² (143mi²) and is the largest of the Italian lakes.
- From top to toe Lake Garda measures 50km (30mi) – about 10km (6mi) shorter than Lake Maggiore which is only Italy's biggest lake by name.
- Lake Garda's shoreline is 125km (77mi) long, about 45km (28mi) less than those of Lake Como and Lake Maggiore.
- The lake has a maximum depth of 346m (1131ft). At its deepest point the bed is 281m (919ft) below sea level.
- Of Italy's great lakes Garda does not have any islands of any size; instead there are just five islets.
- The River Sarco feeds Lake Garda from the north, while the River Mincio flows out to the south.

History, Fact & Fiction

From the prehistoric pile dwellings of the first settlers on the lake to the arrival of the first tourists in the 19th century, the history of Lake Garda and the surrounding area includes many interesting facts. One of these is about the founding of the Red Cross.

In 1842 a Turin newspaper, *Il Risorgimento* (The Awakening), alerted Italians to the fact that their country, once the heart of the Roman Empire, was now ruled by foreigners. Spain controlled much of the south, Austria much of the north, while the rest of Italy was in the hands of small factional states. Spurred on by the newspaper, Italians yearned for the unification of their country but this was to take many years and cost many lives – a great number of those being lost in two major battles fought in 1859 close to Lake Garda's southern shore.

On 4 June the French defeated the Austrian army at Magenta. The Austrians retreated towards the stronghold they had created around

TIMELINE

4000BC Early Bronze Age settlers living around Brescia.

1000BC Celts and Etruscans move into the area.

300BC The Romans defeat the Gaulish Cisalpine empire and the lakes area becomes part of the Roman Empire. The Roman remains at Sirmione, Brescia and Desenzano are among the finest in northern Italy. Verona's amphitheatre (the Arena), dating from the 1st century, is one of the best examples of its kind outside Rome.

5th century AD The western Roman empire falls and the Lombards settle what is now Lombardy.
Queen Theodolinda of the Lombards is converted to Christianity and makes it the 'state' religion. For her services to the faith the Pope gives Theodolinda a True Nail – one of the nails used in the Crucifixion. It is incorporated into the Iron Crown used at the coronation of the Italian kings and is now in Monza Cathedral.

8th century Charlemagne defeats the Lombards and a Carolingian kingdom is established across the lakes area.

9th/10th centuries Carolingian rule ends. The Lombards retake the area but are replaced first by the Magyars, then by the Saxons.

12th–15th centuries Era of the city states. The della Scala (Scaligeri) family hold Verona and Lake Garda, eventually being replaced by the Venetians. To the west the Viscontis and Sforzas of Milan take control.

A place of historical importance: Salò, the largest town on the western side of lake Garda

16th century The Venetians hold Lake Garda, but the land to the west is controlled by the Spanish.

18th century The War of the Spanish Succession (1700–13) ends with Austria controlling Lake Garda and Savoy holding the western lakes. Napoleon frees northern Italy, but Austrian rule is then reimposed.

19th century *Il Risorgimento* unites all Italians in a desire for an Italian state. At a decisive battle in 1859 at Solferino the Austrians are defeated. Finally, in 1870 Italy is unified under King Vittorio Emanuele II.

20th century The Treaty of St Germain cedes Trentino to Italy in 1919. Mussolini signs the 'Pact of Steel' with Hitler (1939), then takes Italy into a war for which she is ill prepared.

In 1943 Mussolini falls from power. Hitler creates the Salò Republic for him on Lake Garda as the new Italian government declares war on Germany.
Partisans execute Mussolini in 1945. The following year King Vittorio Emanuele III abdicates and Italy becomes a republic.
The Treaty of Rome in 1957 creates the European Common Market which later evolves into the European Union.

21st century During the economic and political crisis of 2013, Enrico Letta of the Partito Democratico becomes Prime Minister, heading the three major political movements – the centre, centre-left and centre-right. The populist centre-right politician Silvio Berlusconi is convicted of tax fraud and loses his seat in the Senate.

The Magazine

Peschiera del Garda and on 24 June at Solferino, to the south of Sirmione, they lay in wait. Emperor Franz Josef himself led the army: against him were the French under Napoleon III and the Piedmont troops under Vittorio Emanuele II – three crowned heads together on one battlefield. As dawn broke the French attacked the main Austrian force, while the Italians attacked the Austrian right-wing to the south at San Martino, a total of 270,000 men fighting.

Man to Man

The tide of this second battle ebbed and flowed for 15 hours, the stamina of the soldiers being remarkable. But weaponry had improved since the last great land battle in Europe and the carnage was appalling. Some estimates of are 40,000 men dying that day, and all agree that losses exceeded 25,000 men. As night approached the Austrians retreated behind their defences at Peschiera, allowing the French and Italians to claim victory, although it is probable that they had actually lost more men. The suffering of the injured was terrible. In the heat of the Italian summer many lay for hours as the battle continued around them. Then a violent storm soaked those who had somehow survived. Their suffering led the Swiss businessman and humanist Henri Dunant to found the Red Cross as, faced by such a reality, he realised that "Civilisation means providing mutual help, man to man, nation to nation."

Napoleon was so appalled by the destruction that he immediately proposed a peace plan to Franz Josef, the Austrian Emperor. In a treaty signed at Villafranca, now the site of Verona's airport, he secured Lombardy for the 'new' Italy, but left the Austrians in Veneto, much to the disgust and dismay of the people of Piedmont. It was to be another seven years of fighting before Veneto finally fell to Italy.

Wanted Territory

Though Solferino was the bloodiest battle fought near the lakes, it was not the only one. Because of its position on the great Lombardy Plain trade route from the Adriatic (and the east) to the northern Mediterranean (and Europe), the area had been coveted by kings and emperors ever since history was first documented and between 1117 and 1128 Milan fought Como for control of the western plain.

Eventually Como was defeated and sacked. Power on Lake Como passed to Crisopoli, the 'City of Gold', which stood on Isola Comacina, an island near the lake's western shore. It held the lake for Milan, but Como rose to power once again, siding with Frederick Barbarossa in his war with – and defeat of – Milan. When victory was assured, Como took its revenge on Crisopoli, invading and destroying everything, to such an extent that the town never recovered and only a few ruins can be seen today.

Venetian War Galleys on Lake Garda

In the early 15th century Milan was at war with Venice, the Milanese army marching east to besiege Brescia, an outpost of the Serenissima. Unable to relieve the siege by land, the Venetians attempted to do so by water. A fleet

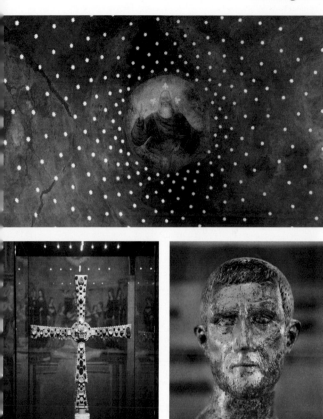

The Museo di Sant Giulia in Brescia traces the history of the Lombards; their former seat of power in Italy has since become a UNESCO World Heritage Site

of galleys, some of them war galleys, others supply ships, were dismantled at Venice, put on ox carts and towed to the River Adige. There the 26 galleys were rebuilt, launched and rowed upstream to Roverto, where they were again dismantled. From here 2,000 oxen were used to haul them to northern Lake Garda across the high San Giovanni Pass. It took three months to get the ships to the lake. By now things were desperate in Brescia and the ships were hastily rebuilt. Still barely serviceable, they were launched and sailed south. At Maderno they were met by a Milanese fleet, hastily constructed there for the purpose. Despite being the superior sailors, the Venetian fleet was not really ready for battle and was defeated. Perhaps it was some consolation to the survivors of the defeat that Venice was to win the war.

FAUNA and FLORA

A wide variety of Mediterranean and sub-tropical plants flourish in the mild climate of the Lake Garda region. However, these have been prevented from spreading as they would otherwise do naturally by the massive intervention of man.

The much-heralded garden and park-like landscape around Lake Garda has little to do with untouched nature as it is much more a cultivated area of fruit trees and vineyards, fig and citrus plantations and olive groves. The once widely spread forests of evergreen holm oaks have now been severely decimated. Ancient beechwoods, however, can still be found today near Prada on Monte Baldo. The evergreen laurel is much more common;

The south in full bloom: in the garden at the Town Hall of Limone on the western side of the lake

the Judas tree on the other hand increasingly rare. Sweet chestnuts ripen at high altitudes. The mulberry bushes were originally planted for silkworm farms. Cypresses and cedars of Lebanon, as well as palm trees and agaves, set picturesque accents in the parks of large villas. Lime trees and maples have been planted to create avenues. Azaleas, oleander bushes, magnolias and acacias fill the air with their scent in the spring and summer. Reed beds and rushes, kingcups, water lilies and water clover can be found in the few flat and marshy areas along the banks of the lake.

The Corna Piana di Brentonico nature reserve on Monte Baldo, which lies at an altitude of between 1276m (4186ft) and 1735m (5692ft), opened in 1972. Preglacial plants have survived, including cobweb saxifrage *(Saxifraga arachnoidea)*, sticky columbine *(Aquilegia thalictrifolia)* and the Dolomite tufted horned rampion *(Physoplexis comosa)*. Endemic plants – i.e. that can only be found here – are the long-stemmed Monte Baldo anemone *(Anemone baldensis)*, South Tyrol cleaver *(Galium baldensis)*,

The Magazine

white-haired Monte Baldo sedge *(Carex baldensis)* and the widow flower *(Knautia baldensis)*. In addition, there are several types of orchid, primula, gentian and lily that bloom between the end of March until May. The Monte Baldo truffle is much-loved by gourmands.

Red and fallow deer, as well as chamois, have now returned to the Parco Alto Garda Bresciano. The Monte Baldo nature reserve is also home to the capercaillie, the rock partridge, the fox and martens. A number of different species of duck, coot and heron have settled in the nature park along the Oglio and Mincio rivers.

The habitat of the reed warblers, little bitterns and river nightingales in marshy areas is becoming increasingly small. Seagulls however have adapted well to the changing environment around Lake Garda. Common redstarts, red kites and ravens live in the rock face. Shrikes, larks and buntings prefer flatter plains.

The rich variety of fish that was once common in the lakes in the Alpine foothills is no longer to be found as a result of pollution. Trout and carp from Lake Garda, however, still reach quite a considerable size and the cisco – a member of the salmon family – that was released into the lake has a acclimatised well. Char, eel, tench, perch, pike and barbel have become quite rare.

Non-venemous snakes live in a few places on the water's edge and, near beaches, they may be seen peeking out of the water, especially in August, or making a quick dash to hide under the nearest stone. There are however poisonous adders on Monte Baldo, although these have become quite rare now, as well as scorpions which can be seen frequently in May and September. Otherwise all sorts of lizards can be seen running up and down the warm stones of walls and, occasionally, you may spot a blindworm too. The variety of butterflies is impressive, especially on Monte Baldo where the range of different flowers provides sufficient food.

Spring produces swathes of colour: gentians on Monte Baldo (below); right: poppies in bloom on a slope overlooking Riva del Garda at the northern end of the lake

Culinary
DELIGHTS

The Italian diet is claimed by many doctors to be one of the healthiest in Europe. The essence of the cuisine is simplicity – good-quality ingredients prepared with the minimum of fuss. Sauces and dressings are, in general, kept to a minimum, with the cooking allowing the ingredients to speak for themselves.

A romantic picnic: *bella Italia*

Pasta and Rice

The basis of many meals is, of course, pasta, but there is also a surprising amount of rice eaten as there are extensive rice fields close to Padua, south of Milan, and near Venice. The best known rice dishes are *risotto alla milanese*, rice with saffron, and *risotto alla monzese*, with minced meat and tomato added. Mantova also has a risotto speciality, a rich mix of rice, butter and onions, while a popular form in the Veneto region is *risotto nero*, rice coloured (and flavoured) with squid ink.

Pasta comes in a bewildering variety of forms, each with its own name. To the uninitiated, the array of shapes seems over-the-top – surely, if they are all made from the same ingredients, they must taste the same? But no, they don't – although the differences are subtle. Basically, there are two types of pasta made either of flour and water or flour and egg. The different grain used for the flour and the ratio of the surface area to the volume – which varies with the shape – results in the number of different types of pasta. Whatever the pasta, there will be a sauce, the most popular being *al pomodoro*, with tomatoes, *alla carbonara*, with bacon or ham and eggs, *alle vongole*, with clams and *alla bolognese*, with minced meat, herbs and vegetables.

As a change from pasta and rice you could try polenta, a maize-based dish often served as an accompaniment to meat, as well as an antipasto. There is also gnocchi, made from chestnut flour and mashed potato and usually including egg yolks and pumpkin, or *pizzoccheri*, a very dark pasta (almost black, and occasionally referred to as black pasta) from Valtellina (near Lake Como).

Pizzas
Pizzerias can be found in every town and village. The most popular types of pizza are the simple *margharitta* (with tomato sauce and cheese) and *quattro formaggi*, which often uses local varieties of cheese.

Starters
Local antipasti include *bresaola*, thin-sliced, air-dried, salted beef, and *missoltini*, sun-dried fish.

First Course
Primi include pasta dishes, such as ravioli – a rich ravioli of cheese and butter is a speciality of the Bergamo area – lasagne or minestrone soup, sometimes so thick with vegetables that, with bread, it is a meal in itself.

Main Course
It is no surprise to find fish from the lakes on most menus. There are many types, but the most popular are perch – delicious when fried lightly in olive

Whether *at* or *in* the lake: having fun on Lago di Garda is a question of the mood you are in

Some of the best ice cream on Lake Garda can be found at the Gelateria Cristallo in Bardolino

oil – and trout. Around Lake Garda look out for *carpione*, a trout only found in this area, which is typically fried after being marinated with herbs. Of the meat dishes, *asino* is popular, particularly around Lake Orta and Mantova, although you may wish to remember before you order that donkey meat forms the basis of various stews. *Agnello* (lamb) is also popular and, in the Ossola Valley near Lake Maggiore, *viulin* (salted leg of goat stuffed with herbs and spices) is a speciality. Various forms of *vitello* (veal) will also be on offer, from lighter meals such as thin-sliced veal with wine or lemon to the richer *cotoletta alla milanese* (➤ box p. 23).

Desserts

The Italians make the best ice-cream in the world, but if you want something more substantial there are *amaretti* (macaroons) and the famous Milanese dessert *panettone*, a buttery cake with sultanas and succade.

The name reputedly derives from the failed attempt to make bread by an apprentice chef in 19th-century Milan. When Toni's bread dough failed to rise he added butter and sweet ingredients and desperately passed it off as a dessert. It was a hit and Toni's bread – *panettone* – was born.

And to Drink

Italian wine is graded either DS (*Denominazione Semplice*), with no quality standard, DOC (*Denominazione di Origine Controllata*) or DOCG (*Denominazione di Origine Controllata e Garantita*), the highest standard.

The western shore of Lake Maggiore produces the famous dry, full-bodied red wines Barolo and Barbaresco, and the Franciacorta area around Lake Iseo produces good red wine and a delicious, sparkling white.

ITALIAN OR GERMAN?

One item on most menus is *cotoletta alla milanese*, a veal cutlet fried in breadcrumbs. This is, of course, the Italian equivalent of a *Wienerschnitzel*. The cross-over between Italian and German dishes or, at least, the change from Italian to German names for dishes, becomes more apparent as you head north along the shores of Lake Garda. In Riva, and certainly in villages to the north, you will see many Tyrolean specialities – *gerstensuppe* (barley soup with speck), *gröstl* (beef and potatoes, boiled then sautéed) and various forms of *wurst* (sausage).

From Valtellina, north of Lake Como, come Grumello, Inferno and Sassella, reds as rugged as the local scenery. But the most famous wines from the lakes area are those from Lake Garda's eastern shore: the light dry red Bardolino, the more full-bodied reds of the Valpolicella and the dry white Soave.

Of distilled drinks, those from Lake Como's Abbazia di Piona are the most famous. The monks' Gocce Imperiali (Imperial Drops) herb-based spirit is a potent brew. On Lake Garda, the Salò-distilled *Acqua di cedro* is a brandy made with citron.

After the meal, perhaps a coffee. Cappucino, locally called *cappucio*, is usually served only at breakfast. Asking for it after a meal may elicit a glance that assesses your virility. The traditional coffee is *liscio*, black and strong, and served in a very small cup. The Italians add lots of sugar. There is also *ristretto*, which is even stronger. To tone either down try *lungo*, with hot water, *macchiato,* with a little milk, or *Americano*, the familiar coffee with milk seen throughout Europe.

The alternative to coffee, particularly mid-morning, is hot chocolate. The normal form is so thick that a spoon will stand up in it. If you want to actually drink it, ask for a liquid version.

GRAPPA

This traditional Italian firewater is made from the pressed skins and grapes left over after winemaking. The liquid is fermented, without adding sugar, then distilled into a clear, dry spirit of between 80 and 90 proof. There are dozens of different types of Grappa.

ART & CULTURE

From Antiquity to the modern day. The region's architectural highlight is certainly the magnificent amphitheatre in Verona. However, many of the castles and beautiful churches – some of which reflect the strong influence of Venetian architecture – and the traditional villas built along the shore of Lake Garda in the 19th century, are equally interesting.

A masterpiece of Romanesque architecture: the main portal of the cathedral of Santa Maria Matricolare in Verona

Pre-history (4000BC–1000BC)

Early man did not have the technology to alter the landscape significantly: not until Neolithic (New Stone Age) times did he leave an indelible mark.

On Isola Virginia, an island in Lake Varese (a small lake near the town of Varese, towards Lake Maggiore) there are remains from Neolithic to Bronze Age times. The Ledro lake dwellings also date from the Bronze Age.

Roman (753BC–5th century)

The Romans developed the 'classical' form of architecture of the Greeks, taking their style of columns and tall, open structures, but adapting them to more functional buildings. As an alternative to brick and stone they also developed concrete as a building material. Verona's Arena is one of the finest Roman ruins in Europe. Domestic architecture can be seen in the villa at Desenzano del Garda, while the villa at Sirmione is one of the largest and most palatial ever found. In Brescia the remains of the temple are modest, but they are still a powerful reminder of Roman craftsmanship, while the excavated finds from the Brescia site are an excellent introduction to Roman art.

Lombard (6th–8th centuries)

A Lombard church that has been excavated in the area behind the high altar in San Severo in Lazise is one of the few relics from this period. Beautiful works of Lombard art can be seen in the Museo di Santa Giulia in Brescia. These include the exquisite, jewel-studded 'Desiderius' cross of the last Lombard king who founded the Benedictine convent of San Salvatore Santa Giulia in 753 on the site of a Roman villa. The medieval church of San Salvatore, the Romanesque church of Santa Maria of Solario and Santa Giulia from the 16th century have all been incorporated into today's museum complex with its modern-day cloister.

Carolingian

The church of San Zeno at Bardolino dates in part from the 8th century. One of the oldest churches in Italy, it is among the few survivors from the Carolingian era as later builders often demolished early churches and used the stone for their own buildings.

Romanesque (10th–12th centuries)

The Romanesque style evolved from an amalgamation of Classical and Oriental influences. A Romanesque church façade has a tall, central section and the main entrance, rising to a pointed triangle at the top. To each side there are lower, symmetrical sections with sloping roofs.

Northern Italy has many fine Romanesque buildings, but to see the finest example of Lombard Romanesque architecture, a much less ornamented form, but with the tall central section pierced by a circular window, visit the church of San Zeno Maggiore in Verona. Cremona's *duomo* is another fine example. The old cathedral (the Rotonda or *Duomo Vecchia*) is a very fine example of the early Romanesque style, while Como's Broletto is the best example of a secular Romanesque building.

Gothic (13th–14th centuries)

The flamboyant architecture of the Gothic period was begun by Cistercian monks and rapidly taken up by other orders, and then by the builders of town churches. One of the most important architects was Arnolfo di Cambio. Although he worked in Rome and Florence, his

On Lago di Ledro: the first settlers in the region around Lake Garda lived in lake dwellings built on piles

The Magazine

influence spread north and can be seen in Salò's *duomo* (cathedral), considered by many to be the crowning glory of Late Gothic architecture.

Renaissance (15th–16th centuries)

The Renaissance saw a return to the symmetry and beautiful proportions of Classical architecture. Palladio's Vicenza is as far as you need to travel to see the best of Renaissance architecture, but there are other superb examples closer to the lakes – Bergamo's Piazza Vecchia and Colleoni Chapel, Verona's Piazza dei Signori and the complex of buildings at Castiglione Olona, south of Varese.

Baroque (17th–18th centuries)

The Baroque style, with its flamboyant swirls and scrolls, was a reaction to the austerity of the Reformation. The scrolls even found their way onto Stradivarius' violins but, in architectural terms, one of the finest examples has to be Isola Bella, the work of Angelo Crivelli, although the façade of Bergamo's *duomo* is also a good example. This was added in 1886, way past the end of the true Baroque era which explains its more restrained form.

Neoclassical (19th century)

This was another return to the Classical form, but this time using modern techniques to add curves and domes. The best two examples are on Lake Como – the Tempio Voltiano in the town of Como and the Villa Melzi d'Eryl (by Giocondo Albertolli) in Bellagio.

Art Nouveau (early 20th century)

There is no better place to look than the villas built by Giuseppe Sommaruga at Sarnico on Lake Iseo.

20th/21st century

In the early 20th century, Functionalism, also known as the International Style, emerged as a prevalent answer to the decorative architectural styles of previous eras. The fundamental architectural principle behind this was that it should be possible to deduce a building's function from its appearance. As a contrast to this, the architectural style of the fascist state in Italy had a Neo-Classicist, Imperial Roman leaning. It was not until after World War II that modern architecture found a foothold. The Venetian Carlo Scarpa (1906–78) worked on the interior design of existing buildings. Major works in which his 'critical restoration' *(restauro critico)* can be seen include the conversion of the della Scala castle into the Museo Castelvecchio. The Banca Popolare di Verona (1973–75) was also built to his plans. Pier Luigi Nervi (1891–1979) of Sondrio, one of the most important proponents of the use of reinforced concrete, especially for wide-span structures, designed the Risorgimento Bridge (1966) and the library (1978) in Verona. The Museo d'Arte Moderna e Contemporanea di Trento e Rovereto in Rovereto (2002) is considered one of the most important buildings of the modern day. The museum, just a few miles northeast of Lake Garda, was designed by the star architect Mario Botta from the canton of Ticino in Switzerland.

DID YOU KNOW...?

...that the prediction of a nose-bleed once saved the area? At Desenzano del Garda in 425 Pope Leo I met Attila the Hun who was intent on destroying the area. The Pope told Attila that if he continued his advance on Rome he would suffer a fatal nosebleed. Attila was highly superstitious and terrified – and retreated across the Alps.

Pulcinella, Arlecchino and Balanzone: Commedia dell'Arte figures as a plate decoration

...that Cornello dei Tasso, a tiny hamlet in the Val Brembana, north of Bergamo, is an important place in the history of communications? The Tassa family began a Europe-wide postal service in the late 13th century and have given their name to Tass, the Russian news agency, and to 'taxi' – a private vehicle service they operated for 16th-century Holy Roman Emperors.

...that, at 315m (1030ft), the Cascata del Serio in the Val Seriana to the north of Bergamo is one of Europe's highest waterfalls even although it cannot be seen most of the time? The water is normally diverted to a hydro-electric power station but on certain weekends in July and August it is allowed to flow over the waterfall again. Crowds arrive to watch the water being diverted.

...that the area has its own saint? Carlo Borromeo was born in Arona in 1538. He was a cardinal at 22, and Archbishop of Milan at 26 (although the fact that his uncle

was Pope Pius IV might have helped). It was claimed that Carlo was too ugly to be anything but a saint, but he is renowned for his humanity during an outbreak of the Plague when, at risk to his own health, he helped victims. His prayers were claimed to have ended the outbreak and he was canonised in 1610. He is buried in Milan Cathedral and a gigantic statue of him stands near Arona.

...that the Commedia dell'Arte began here? The improvised comedy with a cast of masked characters began in Bergamo (although not all of these characters originated in Bergamo itself).

...that an underwater nativity can be seen at Laveno on Lake Maggiore each year? Marble statues of Mary, Joseph, the three kings and animals are lowered into the lake. A marble statue of the Baby Jesus is added on 24 December. The ceremony, the origins of which are shrouded in mystery, is floodlit and attracts many visitors.

Viva la Musica

Having given the world the violin it is no surprise that the lakes area – around Lake Garda in particular – has a strong musical tradition.

The Violin

Gasparo de Salò (born at Salò on Lake Garda in 1540) and Andrea Amati of Cremona (c. 1520–80) each have, in their own way, a claim to how the modern violin evolved. Few people, however, will disagree that Antonio Stradivarius (c. 1644–1737), also from Cremona, was the finest violin-maker of them all.

The Composers

Claudio Monteverdi (1567–1643) was born in Cremona and initially came to prominence as a composer of madrigals, his first collection being published in 1590. Together with other composers – such as **Luca Morenzio** who was born near Brescia – Monteverdi alarmed the musical establishment of the day with his use of unprepared dissonances. In 1601 he was appointed Maestro di Cappella at the Gonzaga court at Mantova where he made another imaginative leap, writing what is now recognised as the first opera, *Orfeo*, first performed in 1607. In 1632 Monteverdi became a priest but continued to compose, producing operas in 1641 (*The Return of Ulysses to his Native Land*) and 1642 (*The Coronation of Poppea*). By then he was 75 years old.

Born into a poor family in Bergamo's Città Alta in 1797, **Gaetano Donizetti** was educated at a charitable school that supplied choristers to Bergamo Cathedral. When his musical talent was recognised, he was sent to study music at Bologna. His first opera was produced in Rome when he was only 25 and for the next 20 years he was the darling of the Italian theatre, writing works for opera houses all over the country to great musical acclaim. Only in 1842, when Verdi's *Nabucco* was performed, did Donizetti's pre-eminence begin to decline. But by then his health was also failing and he returned to Bergamo where he died in 1848. There is a memorial to him in the Church of Santa Maria Maggiore.

Mention must also be made of **Giuseppe Verdi** (1813–1901) for, although he was not born in the area, he composed *La Traviata* while staying near Cadenabbia on Lake Como, and set *Rigoletto* close to Mantova. Verdi was also important during the Risorgimento, when his name was seen as a short form for 'Vittorio Emanuele, Re d'Italia' (King of Italy) and 'Viva Verdi' was written on buildings all across the lakes area.

Music in the air: the opera festival in the Arena di Verona

MORE THAN JUST A VIOLIN

The secret of Stradivarius' manufacturing techniques is still debated. It is known that he scoured forests for the perfect tree. He used maple and spruce for the body of his instruments, pear and willow for the neck, but his drying techniques and the ingredients of his varnish are still unknown. Many professional musicians claim there is no such thing as a 'perfect' violin other than one that best suits an individual's performance. Interestingly enough, this is often a Stradivari.

SPORT is
(not just) in the AIR

Lake Garda is a paradise not only for surfers and sailing enthusiasts, but also for cyclists, mountainbikers, hikers and climbers.
It is also the stage for world premieres: in summer 2014, for
instance, for the new electric hightec surfboard 'Waterwolf'.

Swimming, Sailing, Diving

Thanks to its lovely beaches, Lake Garda has long been a popular destination
for northern Europeans looking for somewhere to swim or to do water sports
away from the coastal resorts. There are beaches (*spiaggia*) and bathing
areas (*lido*) all around the lake with a varying array of facilities. As most of
the beaches are pebbly, flip-flops are highly recommended. The water is
exceptionally clean. Lake Garda is also a favourite for sailing enthusiasts
with numbers increasing noticeably at weekends. There are some two
dozen sailing clubs around the lake which also welcome guests. Tourist
offices provide all the information you need about sailing.

Whether windsurfing or kitesurfing – Lake Garda always has something for everyone

There are some good sites for hobby divers – especially off Riva (north shore), Salò (west shore) and Torri del Benaco (east shore), as well as Peschiera and Desenzano (both on the south shore).

Windsurfing & Co.

On Lake Garda, starting before dawn, the *pelèr* (or *suer*) blows from the north. This lasts until around lunchtime when there is a period of relative calm before the *ora* begins to blow from the south, continuing through the afternoon and evening. Such dependable winds are a gift from the gods to anyone wishing to sail or windsurf. The winds are at their best at the northern end of the lake where it narrows and, thanks to the height of the mountain ridges all around, the air is funnelled making conditions even more favourable. For waterskiers the situation is more difficult, as the use of power boats is restricted, particularly near popular bathing and windsurfing areas and in the confined northern section of the lake.

A completely new watersport that celebrated its world premiere in summer 2014 in Brenzone on Lake Garda manages without either the wind or waves. 'Waterwolf' is the brain-child of a mechanical engineer from Bavaria, Germany. A passionate surfer himself, the designer developed an electric surfboard that reaches speeds of up to 25km/h (15mph). Riding across the lake on a board powered by an electric motor is great fun. The new 'e-board' may well trigger a new wave of enthusiasm among watersport fans rather like e-bikes have done for cyclists.

Hiking, Climbing, Cycling

Monte Baldo is a truly unique place. As this mountain ridge was not covered by a glacier during the Ice Age, a number of so-called 'relict plants' survived the long cold period. These include many endemic species. The mountain is now the best-known hiking area on Lake Garda and hikers are so spoilt by its natural beauty and variety that many people do not just come here once but return time and again.

Three peaks, including the 2218m (7277ft)-high Cima Valdritta, accentuate the massif that stretches over a length of 40km (25mi). Its rocky face drops abruptly to the lake to the west whereas, to the east, there are gently sloping mountain pastures. The summit can be reached from Malcesine in the comfort of a cablecar. There are a number of different paths for walkers across the extensive plateau.

The Sentiero del Ventrar, a two-hour circular tour starting from the upper terminus, is popular. It is however only for experienced walkers with a head for heights. Cables have been mounted for greater safety at exposed sections. The views over Lake Garda and

Above: on a high-rope course not far from Torbole; left: on the hiking and mountain-bike trail from the Pregasina Tunnel to Riva

Malcesine are breathtaking – and two benches have even been installed at one viewpoint, inviting hikers to stop for a break.

On the opposite side of the lake, the Parco Alto Garda Bresciano boasts a wide range of hiking trails. In the Valle delle Cartiere easy paths take you along the banks of the bubbling trout stream from Toscolano Maderno to the ruins of several old papermills.

More challenging and with lots of wonderful viewpoints is the six-hour circular hike from Pregàsina which takes you across Cima della Nara and

The Magazine

Cima al Bal. Time and again fantastic views of Lago di Garda – and of its little brother, Lago di Ledro – open up. The passage between the mountain pastures bursting with wild flowers on Prati di Guil and the craggy ridge that links the two peaks it breathtakingly beautiful. However, you can't always take in the panorama as the path is narrow and exposed.

A child-friendly hike follows the Old Ponale Road from the Ledro valley to Lake Garda. The road was first built in 1851 but, for several years now, has only been used by hikers and mountainbikers. It starts at Pregasina or where the old road branches off above the tunnel, some 200m (656ft) before reaching the village. The path winds its way down towards Lake Garda, dropping 300m (985ft) through a series of steep hairpin bends. Still quite a long way up above the water, the route then runs northwards along the west shore towards Riva, parallel to the lake, and passes through several tunnels. To the left, the cliff face rises up almost vertically; to the right it drops down just as steeply to the lake below. Safety railings do not exist everywhere. Torches worn around the head are recommended so that the children can explore the dark tunnels and many caves. Riva is reached after about 2½ hours. The lake is rather like a Norwegian fjord at its northern-most point.

There is also a wide spectrum of alternatives open to cycling enthusiasts too. These range from gentle bike tours on level terrain to trips along the shore of the lake and demanding mountain routes. Information and maps are available from all tourist offices (► 38) and the Touring Club Italiano. Attractive mountain trails for cyclists can be found to the north of Lake Garda – especially around Arco, Riva and Torbole. In Torbole a shuttle service is provided to take you to the top of the mountain. The Parco Alto Garda Bresciano mentioned above is a paradise for mountainbikers.

Not least of all, the Lake Garda region is a good climbing area. Arco at the north of the lake is a mecca for freeclimbers and hosts the international championships every year.

Cyclists enjoy perfect conditions for their sport on and near Lake Garda

Finding Your Feet

First Two Hours

Arriving By Air

The northern Italian lakes are well served by air, with seven airports spread across the area, from Malpensa in the west (close to Lake Maggiore) to Venice in the east (which is just an hour's drive from Lake Garda).

Milan Linate Airport

■ With Malpensa, Milan Linate is one of Milan's two main airports. It is **2km (1mi)** from the eastern side of Milan's *autostrada* ring and 7km (4mi) from the city centre (tel: 02 23 23 23; www.milanolinate-airport.com).

■ If you are **approaching the airport from the south** the exit is to your right (as usual), but if you are approaching from the north the exit is to your left, i.e. you exit from the fast lane. This catches many people unawares, especially as the signs come a little late.

■ **Alitalia, British Airways and bmi baby fly to Linate**, as does **easyJet**, which has flights from London Gatwick and Heathrow airports.

■ All major international and domestic **car-hire firms** are represented.

■ If you are **driving to lakes Orta, Maggiore, Lugano** or **Como**, it is best to join the *autostrada* heading south (towards Bologna and Genoa), following the ring past the A1, A7 and A4 exits to join the A8 heading north. The A8 will take you to Varese, the A8/A26 to western Lake Maggiore and Lake Orta. Exit at Sesto Calende (Sesto C) to reach eastern Maggiore.

■ For **Lugano and Como**, follow the A9 from the A8. If you use the *autostrade* to enter Switzerland remember that a *carnet* is needed.

■ If you are heading for **Bergamo, Brescia, Verona** or **Lake Garda**, head north on the Milan ring *autostrada* and then follow the A4 towards Venice.

■ If you are **travelling by train** from the airport you will need to get to Milan first. The easiest way to do this is on City Bus 73 – go out of the main exit and bear slightly left. You must buy your ticket before boarding the bus: they are available from kiosks inside the airport (€1.50). The bus terminates at San Babila after about 25 minutes. From here take the metro to Stazione Centrale.

■ The **Star Fly bus** operates directly from the airport to the Stazione Centrale. It leaves every 30 minutes and takes about the same time. The fare (€4) is payable on the bus.

■ There are **taxi services** from the airport but they are expensive.

Milan Malpensa Airport

■ Malpensa is situated close to Gallarate, to the south of Lake Maggiore. It is **6km (4mi)** from the A8 *autostrada* and 50km (30mi) from Milan city centre (tel: 02 23 23 23; www.milanomalpensa-airport.com).

■ Many major airlines fly to Malpensa, including Alitalia, British Airways, easyJet and flybe.

■ All major international and domestic **car-hire firms** are represented.

■ There is a **railway connection**, the Malpensa Express, between Terminal 1 and Milan's Stazione Centrale as well as Cadorna. The journey takes about 45 minutes and costs €11 at the ticket office. Trains run every half-hour all day. From Terminal 1 and 2 there is also a bus, the Malpensa Shuttle Air Pullman, to the centre. It costs €10 but takes an hour. The bus leaves every 30 minutes and terminates at the main railway station.

■ There are **shuttle buses** between Malpensa and Linate.

Bergamo Orio al Serio

- **Ryanair** flies to Orio al Serio from Luton and Stansted, **JET2** flies here from Belfast, Edinburgh and Manchester.
- The airport is **5km (3mi)** southeast of the city and close to the A4 *autostrada* (tel: 035 32 04 02; www.sacbo.it).
- All major international and domestic **car-hire firms** are represented.
- **Buses** run from outside the main arrivals exit to the main railway station in Bergamo. Tickets cost €2.
- There are also **buses to Brescia and Milan**.

Brescia Gabriele D'Annunzio

- **Ryanair** flies to Gabriele D'Annunzio from London Stansted.
- The airport is **20km (12mi)** southeast of the city, near Montichiari (tel: 030 9 65 65 99; www.aeroportobrescia.it).
- All major international and domestic **car-hire firms** are represented.
- **Buses, which connect with Ryanair flights,** run from the airport (outside the main arrivals exit) to the city bus station (stop 24) and railway station. The buses take 30 minutes and cost €6. There are also buses to Verona's railway station. These take about an hour and cost €11 (€16 return). Tickets must be purchased inside the terminal.
- **Taxis** are available for a direct transfer to the city or to Desenzano del Garda. The latter cost about €35 and take about 35 minutes.

Verona Valerio Catullo at Villafranca

- **British Airways** flies to Villafranca from London Gatwick.
- The airport is **8km (5mi)** northwest of the city (tel: 045 8 09 56; www. aeroportoverona.it). There is reasonable access to the A22 (and from it to the A4 *autostrada*).
- All major international and domestic **car-hire firms** are represented.
- **Buses** leave the airport every 20 minutes for Verona's Porta Nuova railway station. The journey takes about 15 minutes and costs €6.
- **Taxis** to the railway station cost about €16 during the day, €18–€19 at night. They take about the same time as buses.

Treviso Ancillotto

- **Ryanair** flies to Treviso from London Stansted.
- The airport is **5km (3mi)** west of the city (tel: 04 22 31 51 11; www. trevisoairport.it).
- Ryanair operates a **bus service** between the airport and Piazza Roma, Venice, costing €7 (€13 return). It takes about 40 minutes.
- **Bus No. 6** connects the airport to Treviso railway station and the city centre. It takes about 15 minutes and costs €2. From the railway station there are trains to Venice every 30 minutes from 5am to 11:45pm.
- Treviso is well located if you are **hiring a car**. Follow the N13 south towards Venice to connect with the A4.

Venice Marco Polo

- Tel: 04 12 60 61 11; www.veniceairport.it
- **British Airways, bmi baby and easyJet** all fly to Marco Polo from London Heathrow, Manchester and Bristol, **JET2** flies here from Leeds and Manchester.
- Transport by **bus** and **waterbus** to Venice is well organised. If you are heading for the lakes your options are more limited. Buses run every

Finding Your Feet

15 minutes to Mestre railway station, from where trains connect to points westward. The journey takes about 20 minutes and costs €3.
- All the major international and domestic **car-hire companies** are at Marco Polo.
- There is reasonable access to the **A4** *autostrada* from the airport.

Arriving By Road
- If you are arriving by road you will either cross the Brenner Pass from Innsbruck, following the A22 to northern Lake Garda and Verona, cross the St Gotthard Pass from Lucerne to reach Lake Lugano and the A9 to Como, or cross the Simplon Pass from the Swiss Valais to reach Domodossola and lakes Orta and Maggiore.

Arriving By Train
- Trains, often night-sleepers, operate from all main European cities to both Milan and Venice and each city has connections to Verona and local stations.

Arriving By Coach
- Eurolines operates long-distance coach services between 31 major European cities, including London, Frankfurt, Hamburg, Milan and Venice.

Tourist Information Offices
The main tourist offices are at:

Lombardy
➕ Via Marconi 1, Milan (beside the *duomo*)
☎ 02 72 52 43 01; www.milanoinfotourist.it
This is the main tourist office for Milan and the Lombardy region.

➕ Via Tasso 8, Bergamo
☎ 035 38 71 11; www.apt.bergamo.it

➕ Piazza Loggia 6, Brescia
☎ 030 2 40 03 57; www.bresciaholiday.com

➕ Piazza Cavour 17, Como
☎ 031 33 00 11; www.lakecomo.com

➕ Via Carobbio 2, Varese
☎ 03 32 28 36 04; www.vareselandoftourism.it

Piedmont
➕ Corso Cavour 2, Novara
☎ 03 21 37 84 43; www.piemonteitalia.eu/de

Trentino/Alto Adige
➕ Via Romagnosi 11, Trento
☎ 04 64 44 31 11
This is the main office;
the following address is better for information on Lake Garda:
➕ Piazza Medaglie d'Oro 8, Riva del Garda
☎ 04 64 55 44 44

Veneto
🛈 Piazza XXV Aprile (main railway station), Verona; ☎ 045 8 00 08 61; www.tourism.verona.it

All towns and most villages also have a tourist office covering the local area. Most of these offices are open seasonally and so may have limited hours or be closed from November to March. Remember that unlike most European countries, you do NOT drop the first 0 when dialling Italy from abroad from a land line.

Getting Around

Bus Services
■ Bus services operate on the **shore roads** of all the major lakes and along the eastern shore of Lake Orta. The services are good, but infrequent on the smaller lakes.
■ On **Lake Garda** bus no. 80 links Riva del Garda with Desenzano del Garda, while buses 62 and 64 link Riva del Garda and Verona. No. 26 runs from Brescia via Desenzano and Sirmione to Verona and back.

Taxis
■ Taxis are **expensive** and are not usually a first option for long journeys.
■ They are **metered**, but it is worth asking what the final price will be before you get in.
■ There are **taxi ranks** in all main towns and local companies post advertisements in hotels.

Rail
■ **Fast and efficient** railways link the cities of the Lombardy Plain. From the cities, branch lines serve the eastern shore of Lake Orta, the western shore of Lake Maggiore as far as the River Toce, the eastern shore of Lake Maggiore all the way to Switzerland, the eastern shore of Lake Lecco/Lake Como, and the eastern shore of Lake Iseo.
■ **Lake Lugano is poorly served**, as is Lake Garda, which has stations only at Desenzano and Peschiera.

Lake Steamers
■ All six of the large lakes (Orta, Maggiore, Lugano, Como, Iseo and Garda), have **steamer services linking the main towns**. The summer and winter schedules vary (with fewer services in winter) so consult local timetables which are posted at all steamer quays or see under: www.navlaghi.it
■ As a general rule there are **commuter services** to and from the main towns early in the morning and late in the afternoon.
■ There are **two types of steamer**. The usual form is a diesel-engined ship that makes a slow journey around the lake. The faster hydrofoils (*aliscafo*) run less often and visit fewer places.

Ferries
■ Car ferries operate on the **three large lakes** with services to the following towns: Verbania and Laveno on Lake Maggiore, Menaggio, Varenna and Bellagio on Lake Como, and Toscalano Maderno and Torri del Benaco (and between Limone and Malcesine in summer) on Lake Garda.

Finding Your Feet

- The ferries **shuttle back and forth** across the lakes and run approximately every half-hour in the high season.
- The **cost depends on the size of car and number of passengers**, but it is very reasonable compared with the time and cost of driving around.

Driving

- Italian roads are excellent. **Sections of the *autostrade*** are two-lane which means they can become congested if slow-moving lorries form convoys.
- The **lake roads** are good, although care is needed in places, for instance the eastern shore of Lake Maggiore, the road from Como to Bellagio and the parts of the eastern shore of Lake Garda where the roads are narrow.
- Be careful of **local drivers** travelling at speed and lane discipline, particularly in urban areas, can be poor.
- If you go into **Switzerland** and drive on the motorways (green signs) you must buy a Swiss motorway tax sticker. To avoid the motorways follow the blue signs to your destination.

Driving Essentials

- Drive on the **right-hand side** of the road.
- The wearing of **seat belts** in both the front and rear seats is obligatory.
- An appropriate harness system for **children aged 3–12** is obligatory.
- **Children under 4** must be in an appropriate child safety seat.
- **Children aged between 4 and 12** must travel in the rear seats.
- The use of **hand-held mobile telephones** while driving is prohibited.
- It is obligatory for **motorcyclists** to wear crash helmets.
- Car drivers must carry a **warning triangle and spare bulbs**, as well as a fluorescent waistcoat for use in emergencies.
- UK travellers must fit **headlight deflectors**.
- **Dipped headlights** must be on at all times outside built-up areas.
- The **speed limi**t on *autostrade* is 130kph (80mph). On main roads it is 110kph (70mph), on minor roads 90kph (60mph). In urban areas the limit is 50kph (30mph).
- There is random **breath testing**. The alcohol limit is 80 micrograms/100ml. Fines are severe.
- **Parking offences** in built-up areas result in on-the-spot fines. You will not be allowed to move your vehicle until it is paid.
- **Tolls** are paid on Italian *autostrade*. Collect a ticket when you get onto the motorway and pay at the booths as you exit. Tolls can be paid in cash (sometimes by throwing coins into a catch net, but there is always an attendant), by credit card or by VIACARD. The latter is of little interest to tourists unless you are travelling a long way or intend using the motorways often.
- There are a good number of **service stations** on the motorways, varying from simple ones selling fuel and refreshments and with toilets, to grander buildings that include shops and restaurants.

Bringing Your Own Car

To bring your own car you will need:

- A **valid driving licence and** the **original vehicle registration form**.
- A **green card** and original insurance cover note. Although in principle a green card is not needed as Italy is part of the EU, the Italian authorities require one to be carried.
- The Automobile Club Italia (ACI) operates a **breakdown service**, tel: 80 31 16.

Accommodation

This guide recommends a cross-section of places to stay. Standards of accommodation in Italy are generally very high and prices – especially at peak times in the holiday season in Italy around *Ferragosto* (15 Aug) – are comparable with those in other north European countries.

Booking a Hotel

- Booking ahead is recommended in high season.
- Travelling without pre-booking is easier in spring and autumn, but note that some hotels are open only during the summer season.
- Most tourist offices have lists of hotels and a few offer a booking service for a small fee.

Italian Hotel Ratings

- The Italian classification of hotels is based on specific features rather than by overall standard. A swimming pool might make a three star into a four, while the absence of a pool might drop a four star to a three.

Rates

- The rate quoted will be for the room, not per person.
- Rates vary with the season. Out of high season and late in the day it might be possible to negotiate a lower rate, but you should not assume this will be the case.
- Rates may or may not include breakfast. Check whether the quoted rate is *con colazione* (with breakfast) and, if not, how much breakfast costs and what it consists of. In larger, more expensive hotels the breakfast will be a buffet and almost certainly worth the money, but at some of the small, inexpensive hotels it might well be limited to bread, croissant and coffee. The local bar might offer the same more cheaply.
- In lakeside hotels there is usually a premium for lake-view rooms.

Rooms for Rent

- Rooms for rent are a popular form of accommodation, particularly in the Lake Garda area, where the sign *Zimmer (camere)* (rooms) is often seen.
- Renting a room for a night or two has great advantages if you want to look beyond the tourist veneer for a more genuine Italy. Families who rent rooms are usually extremely friendly and are often willing to cook dinner.

Camping

- Camping is popular in Italy but varies from lake to lake.
- Lake Orta has no lakeside sites, although there are a few away from the lake near Orta San Giulio and Pettenasco.
- There is a limited number of campsites around Lake Maggiore, with good ones near Maccagno on the eastern shore and Baveno on the

---

Prices

Expect to pay per double room, per night, usually including breakfast:

€ under €80   €€ €80–€130   €€€ over €130

western shore. There are very few around Lake Como and those that exist are away from the lake. There are also few around Lake Iseo. However, the eastern shore of Lake Garda is virtually one long campsite. The sites here vary from the good to the excellent and cater for everyone.

Food & Drink

Italian cooking (➤ 20) is one of the great joys of travelling to the country. As a general rule, whatever grade of restaurant you choose the food will be both well cooked and well presented.

Specialities
- ■ *Pasta*, but also a surprising amount of rice dishes.
- ■ Lake (freshwater) **fish**.
- ■ **Meat specialities**, particularly in the mountain areas above the lakes, where rabbit and other game dishes are popular.
- ■ **Local wines** include Barolo, Bardolino and Valpolicella.

Places to Eat
The difference between a *pizzeria*, a *trattoria* and a *ristorante* are sometimes blurred.
- ■ In general, *pizzerie* are inexpensive establishments serving a variety of pizzas, some pasta dishes and there may well be a salad bar too.
- ■ *Trattorie* have a more extensive menu, but both the menu and the food will be 'no frills'. It will however be well prepared and well served.
- ■ *Ristoranti* tend to have the most extensive menus with wider choices.

Tips
- ■ Most restaurants add *pane e coperto* (bread and cover) to the bill.
- ■ It is normal to **add a tip** as well as paying the *coperto*.

Eating Times
- ■ The Italians eat a **light breakfast** between 7 and 9 in the morning.
- ■ At **lunchtime** many shops close for an extended period to avoid working in the heat of the day. Lunches are leisurely and may last from 12 to 2.
- ■ **Dinner** is the main meal of the day, eaten from 7pm onwards.

Drinks
- ■ Request sparkling mineral water *(gastato* or *con gas)* or still mineral water *(naturale* or *senza gas)*.
- ■ **Wine** is usually drunk with lunch and dinner. Local wines are good value as the restaurant is likely to have a partnership with a local *cantina*.
- ■ **Coffee** is usually served after the meal in various forms.

Prices
Expect to pay for a three-course meal for one, excluding drinks and service
€ under €30   €€ €30–€60   €€€ over €60

Bars

■ If you want a cup of coffee during the day try a **local bar**. Standing at the bar is known as *al banco*; prices are higher if you sit down.

■ In bars it is usual to pay for your drink first at the cash desk. The cashier will give you a **purchase ticket** which you then hand to the waiter behind the bar who will make your drink.

Shopping

Leather is an Italian speciality – shoes, handbags and jackets being of the highest quality. Lake Como – and particularly the cities of Como and Bellagio – are famous for silk. Bardolino and Valpolicella in the east and Barolo in the west are famous wine-growing areas, and Lake Garda especially is famous for its olive oil.

Flea Markets

■ **Bergamo** (Bergamo Alto pedestrian precinct)
Typical fleamarket with all sorts of everything things held every third Sunday in the month (except Aug).

■ **Brescia** (Piazza della Vittoria)
Held on the second Sunday of each month (except in July and Aug); especially good for antiques, furniture and objets d'art.

■ **Como** (Piazza San Fedele)
Held on the first Saturday of each month and good for antiques and objets d'art.

■ **Cremona** (Via Dante Alighieri)
Held on the third Sunday of each month and well-known for furniture and objets d'art.

■ **Mantova** (Piazza Castello)
Held on the third Sunday of each month and good for antiques.

■ **Varese** (Piazza Montegrappa)
Held on the first Sunday of each month and good for antiques and objets d'art.

■ **Verona** (Porta Palio)
Held on the first Sunday of each month and good for antiques, objets d'art and crafts.

Entertainment

As you would expect from an (almost Mediterranean) holiday area, the region around Lake Garda and Verona both have a lively nightlife scene and you can dance until the early hours of the morning in one of the many discos and clubs.

'In' places come and go all the time but the clubs near Desenzano and in Bardolino are especially popular. You can also enjoy the evenings on Lake Garda without spectacular laser or thunderous sound shows. In high season, the lakeside promenades and the Old Towns are atmospherically lit up. Musicians and bands perform on the streets and squares, buskers

Finding Your Feet

show off their talents and restaurant owners are only to happy to serve their customers under the stars until midnight. There are many open-air parties, pop and rock concerts and firework displays – you will certainly not find summer evenings on Lake Garda boring.

Festivals and Events

- **January** On 1.1. at 3pm the traditional *New Year's swim* in the lake takes place in Magugnano (Brenzone) – irrespective of what the weather is like or how cold the water is.
- **February** *Festa di Mezzaquaresima:* This festival is held three weeks before Easter, in the middle of Lent, in Limone. It's not regarded as breaking the fast – religious Christians continue to go without meat – but there is any quantity of fish. And as these 'need to swim', white wine is consumed as well!
- **June** *Festa del Nodo d'Amore:* Tortellini were allegedly invented in Valeggio. For this reason the 600m (1968ft)-long Visconti Bridge is turned into one huge open-air restaurant on the third Tuesday in June. 4000 people come to celebrate the Festa del Nodo d'Amore on the bridge where more than 600,000 *nodi d'amore* – 'love knots' – as tortellini are called in Valeggio, are served.
- **June–September** *Malcesine e l'Europa:* Concerts are held in the summer and plays performed on the beautifully located open-air stage near the castle with its magnificent backdrop.
- **July** *Regatta Bisse:* A late-evening boat race at the southern end of Lake Garda, starting in Bardolino. In keeping with the tradition of the Venetian Republic, rowers stand in their lovely old boats. The historical competition is preceded by a procession of flag throwers.
- **July/August** *The Verona Opera Festival* in the Arena di Verona.
- **August** *Notte di San Lorenzo:* 10 August is a very special night when it 'rains' shooting stars. The whole of Italy gazes at the night sky and, in Peschiera, a big folk festival is staged during the meteor shower, accompanied by delicious things to eat and music.
  Palio delle Contrade is the name of a competition between the different districts of Garda with a canoe race held every year in the evening on 15 August. The teams comprise four rowers to a boat, just like the crews of old in boats used for transporting things and for fishing. The winners of this traditional race with Venetian roots celebrate with a fireworks display.
  Insider Tip Notte d'Incanto: Also on *Ferragosto* (15 August) thousands of floating lights and candles bob around on the lake during the 'night of magic'.
- **September** *Centomiglia:* Every year at the beginning of September, the 'Hundred Mile Regatta' (Centomiglia), the most famous sailing regatta on Lake Garda, starts from the marina in Bogliaco (Gargnano).
  Rock Master: The international freeclimbing championship is held every year in September near Arco.
- **September/October** *Festa dell'Uva:* For more than 60 years a big wine festival has been held on the harbour and lakeside promenade at Bardolino in autumn – the perfect occasion to taste the various Bardolino wines! After dark, there is a fireworks display.
- **November** *Santa Caterina Day:* At the end of November in Castelletto di Brenzone a large festival is held after the olives have been harvested and the first drops of oil have started to flow from the oil presses. You can sample and buy cold-pressed *extra vergine* oil directly from the producers themselves.

Western Lake Garda

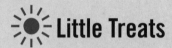 Little Treats

Gaze into the depths

The **'scary terrace'** at Hotel Paradiso in Pieve di Tremosine (➤ 63, 158) drops 400m (1312ft) vertically into the lake below. Pay a visit and test your nerves!

Lighting up the lake

During the **Notte d'Incanto** *Ferragosto* celebrations every year on 15 August in Desenzano (➤ 44, 67) thousands of miniature boats with candles in them bob up and down in the lake.

Floating

Like in the Dead Sea, you can dose off on the surface of the water in Lago della Luna thanks to its high salt content (10%). Perhaps one of the best **spa experiences** on the lake is the 'Lefay' (➤ 69) – which is also open to non-residents.

Getting Your Bearings

The west shore of Lake Garda (Lago di Garda) is often referred to as 'the Italian side' – which isn't really true any more. This was the shore where big villas were built, despite the fact that the terrace between the foot of the risng mountains and the water's edge is narrower here. So narrow, in fact, that on occasions the lakeside road has had to burrow its way through the cliffs that plunge straight into the water.

The famous *Gardesana Occidentale* – for which 74 tunnels were blasted through the rock – leads down the western side of the lake from Riva del Garda in the far north to Salò in the south. Virtually everywhere sheer cliff faces stretch up towards the sky. Nevertheless, there are several lovely places along the route and on the slopes above that all exude a charm of their very own. Among sites worth seeing are magnificent estates such as Vittoriale degli Italiani created by the eccentric writer Gabriele d'Annunzio in Gardone that also boasts another attraction, the Botanic Garden at the Fondazione André Heller. Salò, that adjoins immediately to the south, was turned into the capital of the fascist Repubblica Sociale Italiana for two years under Mussolini. Fortunately, the breathtaking location – one of the most beautiful on the lake – proved to be more enduring that the Republic itself.

Here, too, are Sirmione – very much a 'southern shore' town – perhaps the most picturesque on the lake, Desenzano, with its marvellous old port and Limone where, it is said, the lemons that once made the lake famous were first grown. But the western shore is certainly not just towns and villas. High above Limone and Gardone are the twin plateaus of Tignale and Tremosine where the peace of the countryside contrasts with the comings and goings down on the water's edge.

*It was only after the **Gardesana Occidentale** was built that the settlements on the western shore of the lake developed into tourist centres*

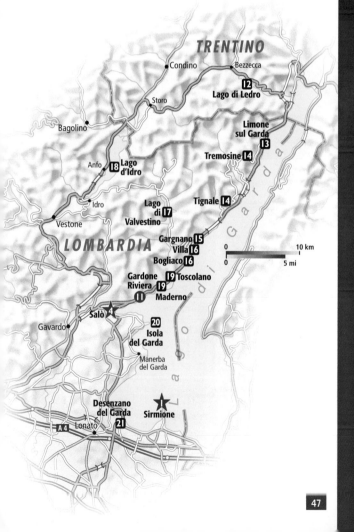

Western Lake Garda

Two Perfect Days

This two-day tour takes in a number of the most interesting places to visit on the west of Lake Garda. For more information see the main entries (➤ 50–68).

Day One

Morning/Lunch
Make an early start from **13 Limone sul Garda** (➤ 62), heading south along the lakeside road for about 6km (4mi) through four tunnels, then turn right to follow the road up on to **Tremosine** and across to **Tignale**. Follow the drive (➤ 158) across the twin plateaus, visiting the church of Madonna di Monte Castello (right, ➤ 63) to enjoy the views and works of art. Now descend past panoramic viewpoints of the lake and the eastern shore – particularly Malcesine and Monte Baldo – to reach the lakeside road again near **15 Gargnano** (➤ 63).

Have a snack at Gargnano, for example at **Bar Azzurra**, Piazza Zanardelli 9.

Afternoon
Head south along the lake road, stopping for a quick look at **19 Toscolano Maderno** (➤ 67) before continuing to **11 Gardone Riviera** and visiting **Il Vittoriale** (➤ 58).

Evening
Relax at one of the lakeside cafés in Gardone, then enjoy the cool of the early evening and stroll along the lakeside promenade. Later, have a meal at the **Trattoria da Marietta** (➤ 70) in Via Montecucco. Stay overnight in Gardone.

Day Two

Morning
Make another early start so you can beat the crowds into ⭐ **Salò** (➤ 55), where the parking can be a problem at the height of the season. One of the highlights is a visit to the *duomo*. On the Lungolago there is a statue to the famous violin maker and double bass player Gasparo da Salò.

Late Morning/Lunch

Between Salò and **21 Desenzano** (➤ 67) enjoy the views of the lake and **20 Isola del Garda** (➤ 67). At Desenzano have lunch at the old port, or on the Piazza Malvezzi nearby where **Ristorante Caffè Italia** at no. 19 is very good.

Afternoon

Now head for ⭐**Sirmione** (➤ 50), just a short drive along the southern shore. Explore the town by following the suggested walk (➤ 156) which takes in most of the historic sites.

In the late afternoon choose one of the many options for a cup of coffee and watch the sunlight reflected on the water.

Evening

Now it's time for a meal, perhaps at the **Trattoria La Fiasca** in Via Santa Maria Maggiore, before a late evening stroll as the first stars appear in the night sky above this incredibly romantic and picturesque place.

★ Sirmione

If you leave the A4 *autostrada* at the Sirmione/San Martino exit or travel along the road that follows the lake's southern shore you will reach Colombare, a pristine if undistinguished village where a road heads off to Sirmione. This 4km (2-mile) drive starts straight-forwardly enough, but soon the peninsula narrows dramatically so that it seems the lake has replaced the roadside verges. Shortly the road widens and reaches a car park (Sirmione is off-limits to all but essential vehicles so you have to leave your car here) and there, ahead of you, is one of the most magical places on the lake.

Entry to the town is by drawbridge and through the gate in the 13th-century walls built by the Scaligeri, the Lords of Verona. Although the Romans were here first, the walls and the castle date from the time of the Scaligeri.

The Castle

The Rocca Scaligera was built by Mastino I della Scala as a garrison and harbour for his fleet of galleys. Dante is reputed to have stayed here and artists by the dozen came to admire it and draw inspiration. The American poet Ezra Pound met the Irish novelist James Joyce here. Although the castle is now empty it is worth a visit for the view from the central tower that rises 27m (89ft) above the lake. The Scaligeri fishtail battlements seen on the walls and towers of the Rocca are a familiar sight around the lake. The museum houses some stone tablets and galleys excavated from the River Oglio.

Sirmione's Rocca Scaligera was built in the 13th century partly of stone and partly of brick to protect the Old Town in the lake

OF LIFE AND LOVE IN ANTIQUITY

Gaius Valerius Catullus (c. 87–54 BC) was born in Verona, went to Rome and rose to fame as a poet. He belonged to a circle of young, progressive poets who took the Hellenistic art of poetry as their benchmark and for whom the scholarly poet was an ideal. From the collection of some 120 poems dedicated to the writer Cornelius Nepos, Catullus' verses on friendship and companionship in particular are notably lively and refreshing. His love poems centred around the female figure Lesbia, alluding to the poetess Sappho from Lesbos, are marked by a personal empathy. His wedding poems in hexameters or elegiac measure are powerfully expressive as are his major epigrams, whereas other texts are characterised by their scathing mockery. In one of his works he calls Sirmione the 'very eye of all peninsulas and isles that in our lakes of silver lie'.

The Grotti di Catullo are the ruins of a Roman villa

Old Town

Beyond the castle the town of Sirmione is crammed into about half the 70ha (173 acres) of the peninsula's head and comprises a maze of alleyways and streets with occasional views of the lake, olive trees or cypresses. To the right, as you head away from the castle, is the **church of Santa Maria Maggiore** from the 15th century. The builders incorporated a Roman capital in the porticoed façade.

Continuing through the town you will reach the **Catullo Spa**, the thermal water that first brought the Romans to the peninsula. Rising from under the lake at a temperature of 69°C (156°F), the sulphurous water is said to be excellent for the treatment of both muscular and sinus problems. The waters are piped to several hotels in the town that offer thermal treatments to guests.

There are places to swim and sunbathe at the head of the island, at the Lido delle Bionde and near the flat limestone terraces at Punta Grotte that extend just above or below the surface of the water around the cape. Some of the best panoramic views of the lake can be had from here, taking in a view to the east and west around the 'belly'

For Protection and Defence

The mighty moated castle of the della Scala family dating from around 1300 is Sirmione's most distinctive landmark and the most important fortified site on Lake Garda.

A fantastic view can be had from the main tower

❶ Masonry: The walls are made of bricks fired locally and natural stone from Cortine Hill nearby.

❷ Gateway and drawbridge: On the gateway you can see where the drawbridge that was once here was closed using a pulley system. The long rods or gaffs disappeared into slits in the wall, as can be seen above the gateway. The pivotal point was in the slits. At the far end there were chains fixed to the bridge. As the inner ends of the beams were pulled downwards, the bridge lifted upwards.

❸ Inner courtyard: The rectangular inner courtyard is surrounded by thick walls.

❹ Tower complex: The corner towers are connected by a *chemin de ronde* – or protective walkway – accessed by a flight of steps. The 47m (154ft)-high main tower, the Mastio, provides wonderful views of the southern end of the lake.

❺ Harbour: The large crenellated castle harbour is unique, not only on Lake Garda but among all European fortresses in Europe. Once used for supplies and defensive purposes, it is now full of water lilies.

Western Lake Garda

and to the north. Surfing is really the preserve of the north, but the lower end of the lake is inviting due to the temperature of the water and is ideal for fair-weather surfers.

Grotte di Catullo

The name may give you the wrong impression as these are not caves nor was it where the poet Catullus lived (see panel ► 51). These are the remains of a representative Roman guest house or the large villa of a wealthy man. The name 'grotte' (lit. caves) was coined by a chronicler during the Renaissance to describe the tumble-down, overgrown complex. At that time it was though that this may have been the site of Catullus's residence. The beautiful location on the white cliffs above Lake Garda and the vast extent of the complex over more than 20,000m² (215,000ft²) – the largest of its kind in Italy – are unique indeed.

The villa was built in 150AD and probably fell into ruin in the 4th century. Ignoring the extensions to the north and south, the main villa is rectangular and measures 167.5 × 105m (550 × 344ft). As the site is not flat, a lower level was constructed under sections of the building, sometimes cutting into the rock. It is largely this basement that can seen today; nothing now remains of the two floors of grand rooms above. Olive trees, rosemary, thyme, mint and oregano now grow among the ruins and emit an intensive smell. In the 2nd century the thermal baths were added in which water from the hot Boiola source was used. There were also probably small shops to the west of the villa.

TAKING A BREAK

The **Bar Ai Cigni** at Vittorio Emanuele 12 is excellent, but the **Gelateria Mancini Da Gino** (Piazza Flaminia 2), serves the best hot chocolate in town.

Insider Tip

✚ 180 C2

Castello Scaligero (Rocca Scaligera)
☎ 030 91 64 68 ◷ Tue–Sun 8:30–7 (outside only) 🎟 €4

Grotte di Catullo and Museo
☎ 030 91 61 57 ◷ March–Oct Tue–Sun 8:30–7; Nov–Feb 8:30–5 🎟 €4

INSIDER INFO

- Sirmione can be **unpleasantly crowded at the height of summer**. It is best to visit before July or after September.
- The **Castello (Rocca Scaligera)** and **Grotte di Catullo** are free to the under 18s and over 65s.
- Near the Catullo Spa is **San Pietro in Mavino**, begun in the 8th century on the site of a temple but rebuilt in about 1000. The church has some good frescoes by the Verona School from the early medieval period. Note *The Last Judgment* (14th century) in particular.

Insider Tip

Salò

The mild climate and beautiful location on a large, gently sweeping bay protected from the wind at the foot of 569m (1867ft)-high Monte San Bartolomeo, where vines, bay and olive trees grow on its slopes, was appreciated by the Romans too.

Under the Romans who called the settlement they founded *Salodium* and the Visconti from Milan, who turned Salò into their administrative seat in the 14th century, as well as under the Venetians (1405–1797), the town developed into the political centre on the western shore and a pivotal point in the region. Later, the mild climate also attracted the aristocracy and the rich from northern Europe. In 1901 an earthquake struck the area. In the years to follow, the old town centre was completely rebuilt and a new lakeside promenade created on wooden piles driven into the bed of the lake.

View of Salò and Monte Baldo on the opposite shore which is often covered in snow well into spring

The Republic of Salò

The town hit the headlines in World War II when it became the seat of the **Repubblica Sociale Italiana** from 1943 until 1945, the last fascist government in Italy, set up with help from the Germans. It started with the arrest of Benito Mussolini in 1943. In a risky undertaking, Hitler ordered Mussolini to be freed from his prison in the Abruzzi and made head of a puppet regime based in Salò and Gargnano. The Ministry of Culture was established in Salò and the Foreign Ministry moved into what is now the Hotel Laurin.

Western Lake Garda

In April 1945, Salò was bombared by the Allies from the eastern shore and, on 29 April, Mussolini fled to Lake Como where he and his mistress were later executed by partisans.

Duomo

Among the maze of squares and narrow streets of the Old Town is the **duomo**, one of the finest late-Gothic buildings on the lake. Inside, the dark stone contrasts with several brilliant paintings, including works by Romanino and Zenon Veronese, and a golden polyptych by Paolo Veneziano. In summer, concerts are given by some of Europe's finest orchestras on the square in front of the cathedral.

Museums

Objects excavated from the Roman *Salodium* are exhibited in Salò's **Museo Civico Archeologico** while the **Museo del Nastro Azzuro**, at

The interior of the cathedral was decorated by artists from Brescia and Venice; the illusionist painting in the nave is by Tommaso Sandrini

> **DID YOU KNOW?**
> *Nastro Azzuro* means 'blue ribbon'. Although the colours of the Italian flag are red, green and white, Italy's national colour is blue: the national football team wears blue and is called the Azzurri, the Blues.

INSIDER INFO

- Salò's **one-way system** is a nightmare if you are trying to park close to the *duomo*. Instead, follow signs for the centre and the hospital where there is a car park nearby. From here it is a short walk to Via Canottieri where new bridges lead to the main promenade and in a few minutes you'll reach the old town and the cathedral.
- If you are **short of time**, simply wander through the Old Town and have a look at the cathedral before stopping for a cup of coffee on the promenade.
- **Pasticceria Vassalli,** at Via San Carlo 84/86, has perhaps the best selection of chocolates on the western shore of the lake. And the most delicious organic ice cream on the lake can be found at **Casa del Dolce** on the cathedral square. *Insider Tip*

Via Fantoni 49, covers the history of the Italian military from Napoleonic times to 1945. One room is devoted to the Salò Republic (▶ 55).

TAKING A BREAK

Salò's lakeside promenade has lots of cafés and restaurants with more in the centre of the Old Town. Try **Bar Posta** at Via Canottieri 16.

✚ 180 B3

Museo Civico Archeologico
✉ Via Fantoni 49 ☎ 33 86 48 21 17
◉ Mon–Fri 10–noon 🖐 €2

Strolling along
Salò's lakeside
promenade

Museo del Nastro Azzuro
✉ Via Fantoni 49 ☎ 03 65 29 07 65
◉ March–Nov Sat, 3–6 🖐 €2

⑪ Gardone Riviera

Tranquil Gardone Riviera was already considered one of the most elegant addresses on Lake Garda in the 19th century and included famous people such as King Farouk of Egypt, the German Emperor Wilhelm II and the Austrian Empress Elisabeth as its guests. Elegant hotels, lavish summer residences and magnificent villas with beautiful park-like grounds still characterise the little town today.

As the slopes of Monte Lavino (907m/2975ft), Pizzocolo (1583m/5194ft) and Monte Spino (1468m/4816ft) come right down virtually to the edge of the lake, the elegant hotels in Gardone Riviera are squeezed along the shore. The old village centre, Gardone Sopra, nestles on a green slope above the Gardesana (Corso Zanardelli). The mountains protect it from the cool Tramontana winds, giving it a Mediterranean climate that made it possible to lay out a beautiful botanic garden. To the south, Gardone and Salò almost merge with each other, with *palazzi* hidden behind the palm trees, cypresses and oleanders that link the two settlements.

The wide but relatively short promenade **Lungolago D'Annunzio**, constructed on piles driven into the bed of the lake, was built after the earthquake in 1901. It is lined

The Neo-Classicist Villa Alba is now a congress centre

The 'stranded' bow of a navy battleship lies in the garden at Il Vittoriale

GABRIELE D'ANNUNZIO: 'INTERPRETER OF HUMAN MADNESS'

Gabriele d'Annunzio (1863–1938) was a prominent, powerfully eloquent Italian poet, a 'war hero' and successful Casanova who called himself an 'interpreter of human madness'. From 1921 until his death, D'Annunzio lived with his wife and several lovers in his whimsical villa on Lake Garda. A few days before acquiring the estate, he was forced to end the illegal, 16-month occupation of Fiume (now Rijeka). Ignoring the ceasefire agreement and supported by a small armed force, he had seized the town that was to be handed over to Yugoslavia at his own instigation in 1919, with the intention of annexing it to Italy. He made an adventurous war-time flight on 9 August 1918, circling his bi-plane over hostile Vienna and dropping propaganda leaflets denigrating Austria. He filled the house and garden of his 'Vittoriale' with military paraphernalia. The most curious of all is the huge bow of the battleship 'Puglia' that was once under his command. The marble mausoleum in the park is, however, the most outlandish evidence of his self-aggrandisement. His sarcophagus, flanked by the marble tombs, arranged like a star, of his wartime comrades from Fiume, lies in the middle of a viewing terrace. Politically he felt close to Mussolini when he was still an unknown Socialist. D'Annunzio's proximity to fascism, his excessive, unconventional lifestyle and his egocentricity cast a shadow over his work as a writer. He published his first volume of poems at the age of 16 and became well-known after the publication of *Il Piacere* (The Child of Pleasure) in 1889 – a novel influenced by Nietzsche. His strength lay in his receptiveness for literary movements and especially for French Symbolism. He confessed his attraction to a heathen cult of the senses and of beauty and, as such, became one of Italy's most controversial lyricists.

Western Lake Garda

with restaurants and cafés
and its northern end is
marked by the jetty belonging to the Grand Hotel
which has a 300m-long
sun terrace right on the
lakeside. This was the first
hotel to be built here in the
1880s. The Piazza Luigi
Wimmer commemorates
the German who introduced
tourism to this side of Lake
Garda and who built the
luxurious Grand Hotel.

**Natural
paradise:
André Heller
describes the
botanic garden
as a
'collection of
flora from
different parts
of the world'**

Visitors to the **Heller Garden** (Giardino Botanico) can
explore a wonderful labyrinth of narrow, twisting paths
leading through the thick vegetation, passing artificially
created streams and lily ponds, crossed by little wooden
bridges. Benches in hidden corners invite visitors to
relax for a few minutes among papyrus, lotus flowers and
bamboo. The park was laid out in 1900 around his villa by
the dentist and natural scientist Arthur Hruska (1880–1971)
of Innsbruck. He planted some 2000 plants from all
climatic zones on earth. The centrepiece of the garden is
a miniature landscape made of stone from the Dolomites.
The Austrian artist André Heller bought the estate in the
1980s as it was starting to get overgrown. The sculptures
in the garden are from him and artist friends like Mimmo
Palladino. The park is divided thematically and starts with
the Asian section, followed by zones focussing on Alpine,
scented and medicinal plants as well as succulents.

From the car park a flight of steps next to the Giardino
Botanico leads up to **Gardone Sopra** and to **Il Vittoriale**.
Gardone Sopra is the tranquil old village centre located on
a slope.

Just before the entrance to Il Vittoriale is the church of
San Nicolà (1740) with wonderful views over the lake to be
had from the terrace outside. The inside boasts several
frescos and a lot of decorative plasterwork.

The complex includes a large park (Il Vittoriale) and the
poet's residence (Casa d'Annunzio). 'Vittoriale degli Italiani'
(The Shrine of Italian Victories) is what d'Annunzio called
the estate that he created more as a whimsical place of self-
adulation than anything else. Visitors first past the open-air
theatre where concerts are held and ballets and plays performed in July and August. In the 'Schifamondo Wing'
(meaning 'disdain of the world') there is a small museum
with photographs, writings and mementoes of the poet and
an auditorium. The SVA plane from which d'Annunzio
dropped propaganda leaflets over Vienna during World War I
is suspended from the ceiling. A path between the main
house and the Schifamondo lead to the park which is scat-
tered with items recalling d'Annunzio's military achievements
and experiences such as the MAS speedboat and the

massive bow of the battleship 'Puglia'. Further up is the gleaming white mausoleum containing the mable sarcophagus with the vain inscription: 'War Hero'. D'Annunzio's house, the so-called Priora (priory), is stuffed full of artworks, kitsch and curiosities and can only be visited on a guided tour.

TAKING A BREAK

It really should be somewhere close to the lake, perhaps **Caffè Wimmer** on the Piazza Wimmer opposite the jetty where the steamer comes in. There are all sorts of places to have a meal in the town itself.

Luxurious oasis: Guests can enjoy the quiet, intimate and very elegant surroundings of the Grand Hotel Gardone located right on the edge of the lake

A180 B3

Il Vittoriale degli Italiani
☎ 03 65 29 65 11; www.vittoriale.it
🅞 Park: April–Se daily 8:0–8; Oct–March 9–5;
Villa: April–Sep Tue–Sun 9:30–7; Oct–March tue–Sun 9–1, 2–5;
Museum: April–Sep Tue–Sun 9:30–7; Oct–March 9–1, 2–5
💶 €8, €13 or €16 depending on the length of the visit

Heller Garden
☎ 336 41 08 77; www.hellergarden.com 🅞 Mid-March–mid-Oct daily 9–7 💶 €9

INSIDER INFO

- To avoid the worst of the **queues** at Il Vittoriale arrive very early or at lunchtime.
- That Italian feeling can best be felt on 🔶 **Rimbalzello beach** at the southern end of the Lungolago. Umbrellas and sunbeds are available for hire.
- Follow the **Barbarano upstream** from Gardone through little gorges with waterfalls and waterwheels which once provided power for a forge nearby.

At Your Leisure

The old harbour in Limone

🔟🔟 Lago di Ledro

Lake Ledro can be reached by taking the well signposted tunnel that by-passes the centre of Riva. During construction work for a hydroelectric pipeline, Bronze Age dwellings were found at the lake where a replica dwelling can be seen at Molina di Ledro, the village at the eastern end of the lake. There is also a museum here (🍴 **Museo delle Palafitte**) that shows how people lived at that time. Beyond

Molina a road hugs the lake's northern shore: follow this and take a more twisty road that stays close to the southern shore to return to Molina. At every point the views are superb.

➕ 180 C/D3

Museo delle Palafitte

☎ 04 64 50 81 82 🕐 July–Aug daily 9–6; March–June and Sep–Nov Tue–Sun 9–5 💶 €3.50

🔟🔟 Limone sul Garda

Limone once boasted the most extensive lemon groves in the whole region. The reputation of this tourist honeypot on Lake Garda is however not due to the fruit but its beautiful Old Town and unique location. Its name in fact almost certainly derives from the Roman word *limes*, meaning a border – Limone having once been a border town between Italy and Austria. Lemons and also citrons – a lemon-like fruit used in the production of *acqua di cedro*, a lemon brandy – and other citrus fruits were grown on terraces above the lake; the trees being enclosed in greenhouses during the winter to protect them from frost. With the unification of Italy, Sicily soon

Map labels:
Lago di Ledro 🔟🔟 Limone sul Garda 🔟🔟
Lago d'Idro 🔟🔟 Tremosine 🔟🔟
Lago di Valvestino 🔟🔟 Tignale 🔟🔟
Gardone Riviera 🔟🔟 Gargnano 🔟🔟
Villa & Bogliaco 🔟🔟
Toscolano–Maderno 🔟🔟
Salò ⭐ Isola del Garda 🔟🔟
Sirmione ⭐
Desenzano del Garda

replaced Limone as the chief producer of lemons and now little remains of the old terraces.

Limone hit the headlines in 1979 when Professor Cesare Sirtori of Milan discovered an unusual protein, called the Apolipoprotein A1 Milano, a gene that rids the arteries of fats and so virtually eliminates arteriosclerosis and heart disease. To date, this gene has only been found among the residents of Limone – in the blood of one single local family – and passed on from one generation to the next. As a result, Limone has the highest concentration of over-80s in the whole of Italy.

The coming of the *Gardesana Occidentale* ensured Sirmione's development as a tourist resort – up until 1931 it could only be reached by boat. The wide lakeside prome-nade, Lungolago Marconi, lined by numerous souvenir shops, cafés and bars, leads to the Piazza Garibaldi at the centre. Just a few yards further on, the old harbour – a small basin surrounded by buildings smothered with flowers – comes as a surprise. You can either stroll along the generally crowded main streets near the shore where shops and cafés rub shoulders with each other, or climb the steeper, twisting little alleyways up the slope where you will find quiet squares, low archways and ivy-clad façades.

➕ 181 D4

🔢 Tremosine and Tignale ^{Insider Tip}

High above the lake, between Limone and Gargnano further to the south, are Tremosine and Tignale plateaux where flower-filled meadows, wooded slopes, rock faces, high hills and small villages combine to make one of the most beautiful areas on Lake Garda. This is a region to be explored on a leisurely drive (➤ 158) or even on foot, but if you only have a short time choose a day when the air is clear and take the road to

The church of Madonna di Monte Castello, near Tignale

Tignale off the Gardesana Occidentale to the north of Gargnano.

There are a number of view points along this road from which the lake and Monte Baldo can be admired. A few miles further on, a short, steep road leads to the church of **Madonna di Monte Castello**, built on the ruins of a Scaligeri castle and famed for its view and works of art. These include four paintings on copper attributed to Palma the Younger and a fresco of the Madonna and Child that some authorities claim is by Giotto.

➕ 180 C4 (Tignale) D4 (Tremosine)

Madonna di Monte Castello
➕ 180 C4 (at Tignale) ☎ 036 57 30 19
🕐 Easter–Oct daily 9:30–7 🎫 Free

🔢 Gargnano

The tiny centre of this former fishing village of twisting streets surrounds a little harbour and a short lakeside promenade with the obligatory cafés and *trattoria*. To the north of the centre, on the Gardesana, is the parish church of San Martino that was built in 1837 in the Italian Classicist style. A huge eliptical inner room opens up behind a portico. Narrow lanes lead down to the lake and the pretty little harbour. During the Risorgimento (1866), French and Italian ships retreated to this spot and were bombarded from the lake by six Austrian gunboats. The scars caused at that time can still be seen on the 16th-century Palazzo Comunale (the old town hall) near the harbour.

Gargnano came to the attention of the world public once again from 1943 until 1945 when Germany sought to establish a puppet regime under Benito Mussolini. Mussolini ruled the 'Republic of Salò' (► 55) from his office in the Palazzo Feltrinelli at the northern end of the lakeside promenade. The Neo-Renaissance palace is now owned by the University of Milan which holds language courses for foreigners here. Just a little further on is La Fontanella park with a pebbly beach and concrete platforms for sunbathing and swimming.

Beyond – actually in Faustino – is the former summer residence of the Feltrinelli family which made a fortune in timber and publishing. It is now a stylish luxury hotel. The church of **San Francesco**, with its single nave, lies to the south of the harbour

in the Via Roma. The Franciscan order established a house of prayer and monastery here from 1289 onwards, of which only the façade of the church and the cloisters have survived, while the church was given its present appearance in the 17th century. The Romanesque and Late Gothic cloister is delightful; its delicate columns support capitals with different and imaginative ornamental elements, including citrus fruit and animals. The church is seldom and irregularly open. You are most likely to be lucky if you come on a Sunday.
✚ 180 C3

Church of San Francesco and Cloister
☎ 036 57 10 17 ⊙ Daily 8–8 💷 Free

🔟 Villa & Bogliaco
There are twelve other little settlements that go to make up Gargnano, including Villa and Bogliaco that link up to the south along the shore. The other hamlets cling to the slope above the main village. One house on the main lane in Villa was where the English writer D.H. Lawrence (1885–1930) lived and worked for a year. From San Tommaso's church above, there is a lovely view of the lake.

The most prominent building in Bogliaco is the Palazzo Bettoni (not open to the public). The magnificent, three-winged palace with an impressive façade overlooking the lake, has been cut off from its park by the through road. Modelled on the Palace of Schönbrunn in Vienna, it was built around 1750 for Conte Giovanni Bettoni, a general in the calvary in the service of Maria Theresia. Bogliaco has a beautiful golf course, founded in 1912, then only the third in Italy (www.golfbogliaco.com). A little further south is the modern Marina di Bogliaco.
✚ 180 C3

Paradise has a name: Gargnano

Pure luxury: One does not merely stay in the Villa Feltrinelli – one resides here!

17 Lago di Valvestino

From Gargnano a road winds up through a series of hairpin bends away from Lake Garda to Val Toscolano and Lago di Valvestino, a man-made reservoir, that often lies shrouded in clouds in the mountain valley. From the lake's far end the valley leads northwards. There are no places to go for a swim but, climbing steeply to the village of Magasa, you will reach the perfect place from which to start beautiful hikes through this dramatic, scenic landscape.

180 C4

18 Lago d'Idro

Continuing westwards from Lago di Valvestino, or heading through the lovely Val Sabbia from Salò, you will reach the town of Idro which shares its name with the little lake on which it stands. Have a look at the church of San Michele, with its finely carved high altar, the organ case and the choristers' seats in the choir. From Idro, a road follows the eastern edge of the lake to the

village of Vesta where it ends. The views from here to the foothills of the Alps are superb.

On the western side of the lake the road burrows its way through the hills to Anfo. The privately owned castle was Giuseppe Garibaldi's headquarters during his campaign to add Veneto to the kingdom of Italy. The church of **San Antonio** has a 12th-century *campanile* and excellent Renaissance frescoes.

180 B4

🔟 Toscolano-Maderno

The little town of Toscolano-Maderno on the western shore of Lake Garda is made up of two settlements divided by the mouth of the River Toscolano – Maderno to the south and Toscolano to the north. With its crescent-shaped bay, long lakeside promenade and attractive villas, as well as an old town centre and harbour, Maderno definitely has more to offer than Toscolano that is really only appealing to campers staying on the site to the north. Maderno is the western terminus for Garda's car ferry (to Torri del Benaco).

One attraction in the twin-town is the Orto Botanico Ghirardi with glasshouses full of tropical plants. On the Piazza San Marco near the harbour is the noteworthy Romanesque church of **Sant'Andrea Apostolo**, built in 1140, with a Late Gothic *campanile* (1469). To the left of the church is the Via Benamati that leads through the Old Town to the River Toscolano, passing the ruins of a Roman villa (no. 79) with a flight of steps set in an enchanting garden. The parish church of Sant'Ercolano is just a few yards further on. It was built on the site of a fortress in the mid 18th century and its tower was converted into a belltower.

➕ 180 C3

Orto Botanico Ghirardi
✉ Via Religione
☎ 03 65 64 12 46 or 02 5031 48 63
🕐 May–Sep Wed, Fri 4:30–8 💶 Free

🔟 Isola del Garda

Just off the San Fermo promontory, the 1km (0.6mi)-long Isola del Garda – the largest island on Lake Garda – rises out of the water. It is privately owned by the Borghese-

Opposite: A jewel on Lake Garda – the villa of the Counts of Borghese-Cavazza on Isola del Garda

Cavazza family who live in a beautiful villa from the turn of the century, set in the middle of a landscaped park. The island can be visited on a 2-hour guided tour. The history of the island and associated legends are related and the Italian and English gardens visited. St Francis of Assisi allegedly founded a hermitage here in 1221 in whch five monks devoted their lives to contemplation and absolute poverty. The poet Dante Alighieri reputedly visited the island a century later.

➕ 180 C3
🚢 Ferries run May–Oct from Gardone Riviera and Garda to the island. For departure times, see www.isoladelgarda.com
💶 €25, for the crossing, guided tour and refreshments

🔟 Desenzano del Garda

The attractive old harbour basin in this, the largest town on Lake Garda, is separated from the port area by a low bridge. The Venetian Palazzo Todeschini facing the harbour was once a grain store. It now houses the tourist information office. Adjoining the lakeside promenade, Lungolago Cesare Battisti, a large, ornately decorated sarcophagus can be seen that served as a tomb for the Roman Atilia Urbica. The cafés and restaurants

Western Lake Garda

Lago di Ledro **12** Limone
                        sul Garda
Lago   Tremosine **14** **13**
d'Idro **18**
Lago di   **14** Tignale
Valvestino **17**
          15 Gargnano
Gardone   **16** Villa & Bogliaco
Riviera **19** Toscolano–
        11   Maderno
Salò **20**
      Isola
  del Garda
              21 ★ Sirmione
Desenzano
del Garda

right behind the harbour on the Piazza Malvezzi are an inviting place to sit in the shade of the low arcades. The monument in the middle of the square is dedicated to the patron saint of the town, Santa Angela Merici, who founded the Order of St Ursula in 1535. The **Duomo Santa Maria Maddalena**, built by the architect Giulio Todeschini (1524–1603)

in the Late Renaissance style, is on the north side of the *piazza*. The number of large oil paintings inside comes as a surprise. The most important is probably Tiepolo's *Last Supper* (1738) in the Chapel of the Holy Sacrament, the second chapel on the left.

In 1921, the ruins of three Roman buildings were unearthed in the middle of a residential area (Via Crocefisso 22). These included the **Villa Romana**, one of the most beautiful and important of its kind in Upper Italy. The excavated site is especially famous for its mosaic floors, now housed in a museum.
✚ 180 B2

Villa Romana
✉ Via Crocefisso 22
☎ 030 9 14 35 47
🕐 Tue–Fri 8:30–7
💶 €4

Museo Archeologico Rambotti
✉ Santa Maria de Senioribus, Via Anelli
☎ 030 9 99 42 75
🕐 Tue–Fri 3–7, Sat–Sun 2:30–7
💶 Free

Rivoltella is one of the most beautiful beaches in Desenzano; this is where rowers uphold an ancient tradition that was brought here from La Serenissima

Where to...
Stay

Prices
Expect to pay per double room, per night
€ under €80   €€ €80–€130   €€€ over €130

DESENZANO DEL GARDA

Piroscafo €€ *Insider Tip*
Adjacent to the old harbour. The rooms are simple but have air-conditioning and are well-looked after; some have balconies.
🏠 180 B2 ✉ Via Porto Vecchio 11
☎ 030 9 14 11 28; www.hotelpiroscafo.it

GARDONE RIVIERA

Grand Hotel Gardone €€€
One of the lake's grand hotels, with chandeliers, period furnishings and elegant bedrooms, plus a heated outdoor pool and private beach.
🏠 180 B3 ✉ Corso Zanardelli 84
☎ 036 52 02 61; www.grangardone.it
🕐 Closed mid-Oct to April

Monte Baldo €€
Right on the lake. Bright, air-conditioned rooms, three luxury suites in Villa Acquarone – a separate building. Pool, jetty in the lake, restaurant
🏠 180 B3 ✉ Via Zanardelli 110
☎ 036 52 09 51; www.hotelmontebaldo.it
🕐 Closed mid-Oct to April

GARGNANO

Grand Hotel a Villa Feltrinelli €€€
One of the best hotels in Europe with a sophisticated elegance and perfect service – and a helipad for guests.
🏠 180 C3 ✉ Via Rimembranza 38–40
☎ 03 65 79 80 00; www.villafeltrinelli.com

Lefay Resort & Spa €€€
A beautiful resort in the *Limonaia* style high above Gargnano and the lake with magnificent views. Two

outdoor pools, an excellent spa, with one suite on the lake with its own private pool.
🏠 180 C3 ✉ Via Feltrinelli 118
☎ 03 65 24 18 00; www.lefayresorts.com

LIMONE SUL GARDA

🛏 Lido €€
Friendly and comfortable, right on the lake. Half board only.
🏠 181 C4 ✉ Via IV Novembre 34 ☎ 03 65 95 45 74; www.lidohotel.com 🕐 Closed Oct–April

SALÒ

Duomo €€€
Fantastic location, lovely rooms, very good restaurant.
🏠 180 B3 ✉ Lungolago Zanardelli 63
☎ 036 52 10 26; www.hotelduomosalo.it

SIRMIONE

Flaminia €€€
In the Old Town right on the lake. Lovely sun terrace.
🏠 180 C2 ✉ Piazza Flaminia 7
☎ 03 91 60 78; www.hotelflaminia.it

Villa Cortine €€€
Small *grand hôtel* in a beautiful villa with peaceful gardens.
🏠 180 C2 ✉ Viale C. Gennari 2 ☎ 030 9 90 58 90; www.palacehotelvillacortine.com

TREMOSINE

🛏 Village Hotel Lucia €
A hotel and holiday 'village' on the edge of Tremosine.
🏠 180 C4 ✉ Via del Sole 2 ☎ 03 65 95 30 88; www.hotellucia.it 🕐 Closed mid-Oct to March

Where to...
Eat and Drink

Prices
Expect to pay for a three-course meal for one, excluding drinks and service
€ under €30   € €30–€60   €€€ over €60

DESENZANO DEL GARDA

Ristorante Pizzeria Kapperi €€
A modern and spacious pizzeria. Freshly made pasta dishes are a speciality.
➕ 180 B2 ✉ Via N. Sauro 7
☎ 030 9 99 18 93 🕐 Closed Mon

GARDONE RIVIERA

Trattoria da Marietta €€
A short walk from Il Vittoriale, this is an unpretentious and friendly place. Excellent food and a good wine list.
➕ 180 B3 ✉ Via Montecucco 78
☎ 036 52 09 60 🕐 Closed Thu

Villa Fiordaliso €€€
A meal here is one of the great dining experiences on the western shore: wickedly expensive, wickedly good. The restaurant with rooms is in an elegant villa. The cooking, service and wine list are first-class. Booking is essential.
➕ 180 B3 ✉ Corso Zanardelli 150
☎ 036 52 01 58 🕐 Closed Mon and Tue lunch, and mid-Nov to March

GARGNANO

La Tortuga €€€
Michelin-star restaurant on the upper section of the lake.
➕ 180 C3 ✉ Via XXIV. Maggio 5
☎ 036 57 12 51 🕐 Closed Tue

PIEVE DI TREMOSINE

Miralago €€
Possibly the best-positioned restaurant on Lake Garda, on the top of the cliff in Pieve di Tremosine. On a clear day the view is sensational. Straightforward cooking excellently presented. Some dishes include local chestnuts and mushrooms, each of which should be tried.
➕ 180 D4 ✉ Piazza Cozzaglio 2
☎ 03 65 95 30 01
🕐 Closed Thu and mid-Dec to mid-Jan

SALÒ

La Campagnola €€€
Delicious fish from Lake Garda: trout, tench, pike, whitefish.
➕ 180 B3 ✉ Via Brunati 11
☎ 036 52 21 53 🕐 Closed Mon

Osteria di Mezzo €€
On a road that runs parallel to the promenade, two streets back from the town hall, this little restaurant has a simple menu with well-prepared food and friendly service.
➕ 180 B3 ✉ Via di Mezzo 10
☎ 03 65 29 09 66 🕐 Closed Tue

SIRMIONE

Locanda La Noce €
Tucked between Jacky Bar and the Hotel Sole, this is a delightful *spaghetteria* with a terrace and lovely views across the lake.
➕ 180 C2 ✉ Via Monsignor Comboni 33
☎ 03 65 95 40 22 🕐 Closed Wed, Nov–Jan

Trattoria La Fiasca €
You'll find this charming restaurant up a side str eet in Sirmione. Delicious minestrone soup. *Insider Tip*
➕ 180 C2 ✉ Via Santa Maria Maggiore 1
☎ 030 9 90 61 11 🕐 Closed Wed and Feb

Where to…
Shop

Most of the towns and villages on Lake Garda's western shore are small, with limited shopping potential, with the exception of Salò and Desenzano. Cafés, restaurants, souvenir shops and a few conventional outlets dominate the centre of many villages.

DESENZANO DEL GARDA

Cashmere Ironia (Via Porto Vecchio) sells tempting pullovers and scarves from its own production line whereas **Intimamente** (Via Santa Maria) has designer underclothes for men and women.

For jewellery go to **Gioielleria Franzoni** (Via Roma 16). For leather try **Martinetti** (Via Generale Achille Papa 40), particularly for handbags and belts, and **La Bagagerie**, (Via Porto Vecchio 22).

If you are interested in art, try **Galleria La Cornice** (Piazza Giuseppe Malvezzi 45) which has interesting modern artworks in wood, metal and ceramics, as well as paintings on wood.

GARDONE RIVIERA

Enoteca Bedussi (Corso Repubblica 40) sells a large collection of wines, spirits and local liqueurs; **Antique Marino** (Piazza Marconi 6) has a good range of antiques – an unsual find in such a small town.

LIMONE

There is a limited number of shops in the town, the best of which are **Pace Mirella** (Lungolago Marconi 14) for a huge range of dried fruits and nuts, and **Raffi**, on the same street (no. 48), which sells stylish designer clothes.

SALÒ

For handbags and elegant jewellery try **Tranquilli** (Via San Carlo 58), elegant fashions can be found at **MR** (Via S. Carlo 39), and for shoes try **Principe** (Lungolago Zanardelli 21).

GB Argento (Via Fantoni 10) has a superb range of silverware, **Quartiere Chic** (Via Fantoni 1) kitchenware and linens for the home and **Ottica Scotti** (Piazza G Zanardelli 7) gold, silver and crystal.

The best antiques are at **Negoziuo d'Arte da Marinella** (Lungolago Zanardelli 29/30); **Colorificio Nastuzzo** (Via Fantoni 35) sells artists' materials and offers watercolour courses.

SIRMIONE

Clothes and fashion boutiques can be found on the Via Vittorio Emanuele, linking the castle and the Catullo Thermal and a few of the side streets.

Other outlets include **Art Gallery Donavil** (Via Dante 15) for Chinese antiques, English silverware and Murano glass, **L'Enoteca** (Corte Salvelli 6) and **Enoteca Il Volto** (Via Piana 16) which both have a huge range of wines, **Sogni Profumati** (Piazza Castello 12) where there is an amazing collection of soaps, candles and perfumes, and **Più Gioielli**, (Via Vittorio Emanuele 54) for jewellery, particularly amber.

MARKETS

There are good weekly markets at **Desenzano del Garda** (Tue), **Limone** (Tue), **Manerba** (Fri), **Salò** (Sat), **Sirmione** (Fri), **Toscolano Maderno** (Thu).

There is also an excellent antiques market in Desenzano del Garda on the first Sunday of the month (except Aug).

Where to...
Go Out

SPORT AND LEISURE

Watersports
Sailing and **windsurfing schools** can be found in Sirmione (**Martini**, tel: 32 01 11 24 65 and **Lana**, tel: 33 86 24 36 50 are among the best), Desenzano (**Fraglia Vela**, tel: 03 09 14 33 43) and Campione (**Vela Club**, tel: 03 65 91 69 08).

The **Centomiglia Sailing Competition** (www.centomiglia.it), held at Gargnano in September, is one of Europe's premier events and attracts entries from far and wide.

Diving is good at the southern end of the lake and there are several schools in Desenzano, including **Asso Sub Il Pelicano** (tel: 03 09 14 44 49). **Boat hire** is available in most of the lake towns.

Adventure Sports
Hiking on Tremosine-Tignale is wonderful, and the plateaus also offer more adventurous opportunities with **parasailing** and **canyoning**.

Golf
There are few courses on the western shore. The **Club Palazzo Arzaga** (www.palazzoarzaga.com) near

---

FROM THE LAKESIDE TO ALTIPLANO BY MOUNTAINBIKE
You are almost certain to get wobbly knees if you take the mountainbike stretch from the harbour in Campione di Tremosine to Pieve di Termosine up on the plateau. The landscape and route itself are stunning. The tour is 23km (14.3mi) long with an altitude difference of 750m (2460ft) overall, with lots of ups and downs. It takes between 4 and 5 hours.

Padenghe (just north of Desenzano) has 18-hole and 9-hole courses.

Close by, at Soiano del Lago there are 18-hole and 9-hole courses at the **GardaGolf Country Club** (www.gardagolf.it). There is also a 18-hole course at **Bogliaco Golf Resort** (www.golfbogliaco.com) in Toscolano-Maderno.

SPAS

Sirmione has many opportunities for relaxation, not only in its hotels but also at the **Terme di Sirmione, Stabilimento Catullo** at Via Punta Staffalo 1 (tel: 03 09 16 81; www.termedisirmione.com).

FESTIVALS

The **Estate Musicale del Garda Gasparo da Salò** is a classical music festival (July–Sep) with open-air concerts on the Piazza Duomo. Other concerts from July to September are held in Gardone Riviera, Desenzano del Garda and Gargnano. Classical music concerts are also held in Salò's **Palazzo Fantoni** in May and June and an **International Classical Music Festival** takes place in August in Manerba.

A **Guitar Festival** is held each September in Gargnano and a **Jazz Festival** from June to September at Gardone Riviera.

NIGHTLIFE

During the summer there is an **open-air cinema and theatre** in Desenzano in the Castello. The best area for discos and music bars is also in and around Desenzano. Of the discos currently open, the best are **Art Club** (tel: 03 09 12 72 85; www.artclubdisco.com) at Via Mella 4 and **Sesto Senso** (tel: 03 46 21 78 80 04) at Via dal Molin 67 in Desenzano itself, **Dehor** in Via Fornace dei Gorghi 2 (tel: 03 46 21 78 80 04; www.dehor.ne) and **Fura** (tel: 03 09 13 06 52) at Via Lavagnone 13 in Lonato.

Eastern Lake Garda

 **Little Treats**

Weekly markets

The market with the most stands is in
Malcesine (►78). On Saturdays, there is
a huge selection – especially of leather
goods – spread over the whole square in
front of the town hall.

Liquid gold

On St Catherine's Day (25 Nov) the year's
fresh, cold-pressed *extra virgine* olive oil
can be sampled at the producers' stands
during the **olive oil festival** in Castelletto di
Brenzone between Torri del Benaco (►91)
and Malcesine (►78).

That Tuscan feeling

Slender cypress trees, rolling hills and vineyards – the spa hotel **Principe di Lazise** (►93),
arranged around a courtyard, gives you that
unforgettable Tuscan feeling.

Getting Your Bearings

At first glance it might be said that the western shore of Lake Garda, with its beautiful villas, gardens and historic towns, is more for lovers of history and culture, whereas the eastern shore, with its beaches and campsites, appeals more to sun-lovers and the active visitor. There is an element of truth in that, but both sides of the lake have much more – often unexpected things – to offer.

At the southeastern tip of Lake Garda there are classic entertainment sites such as Gardaland and nearby waterparks. But this is also a land of vines, the famous wines of Bardolino being pressed from grapes grown within sight of the lake. Further inland are the vineyards that produce Valpolicella, one of the great wines of Italy. There is history here too. At Peschiera the Austrians built huge fortifications to maintain their grip on this part of the country. The battle at Solferino loosened the Austrians' hold, but the legacy of massive walls remains.

The strategic importance of the lake is also reflected in the castles that pre-date Austrian Peschiera – Scaligeri castles with their familiar fishtail battlements. Lazise is a fine example, but the best is at Malcesine, its tower having become a symbol of the lake. Between the two is Garda, the town which gave its name to the lake, while beyond Malcesine, at the head of the lake, is Riva del Garda, now an important tourist centre but with a castle that hints at a less peaceful past. History certainly has a place on the eastern shore and, if the east does not match the profusion of villas on the west, it has its natural delights – Monte Baldo, above Malcesine, is one of the best and most accessible mountain ridges on the lake. And the many little wonders to the left and right of the routes you pass should not be overseen: namely the region's famous flora. As Monte Baldo was not covered by a glacier in the Ice Age, many 'relict plants' survived the long period of cold, including a number which are unique to the area.

Soaking up the sun in Torri del Benaco that was colonised by the Romans at the same time as Verona

TOP 10

⭐ Malcesine & Monte Baldo ➤ 78
⭐ Garda ➤ 83
⭐ Riva del Garda ➤ 85

At Your Leisure

Two Perfect Days

This suggested route takes you to some of the most interesting sights on the eastern side of Lake Garda in two days. For more information see the main entries (▶ 78–92).

Day One

Morning
Start the morning with a walk around the massive fortifications of **24 Peschiera del Garda** (▶ 88), then take the lakeside road north to **26 Lazise** (▶ 89). Here the old port, with its reminders of the Venetian Republic, and the still impressive Scaligeri castle underline the area's importance in medieval Italy. Have lunch at one of Lazise's harbour restaurants – perhaps **Alla Grotta** which has fine views of the old port.

Afternoon
Continue north to; **Bardolino** (right, ▶ 90), whose vineyards have made the town's name famous. You can visit the wine museum which is also a winery or take a short detour along part of the wine route that leads through the vineyards past many of the finest *cantine*. Later, continue north from Bardolino to reach ⭐ **Garda** (▶ 83).

Evening
After a stop for coffee and a short exploration of the town, drive about 4km (3mi) to **28 Punta di San Vigilio** (▶ 90) to enjoy a swim at one of the most picturesque beaches on the eastern shore. Return to Garda for your evening meal – try the **Casa Lady** in Via Verdi – and then stay overnight in Garda.

Day Two

Morning/Lunch
You could head back to Punta di San Vigilio for an early swim to set you up for the day. Next travel north to **29 Torri del Benaco** (▶ 91) where there is another Scaligeri castle, this one housing a museum that will give you

an insight into local olive oil production: you will soon be passing olive plantations on the flanks of Monte Baldo. Continue to Malcesine but do not go into the town. Instead, head for the cable-car and take the short ride to the mountain-top café for a light lunch.

Early Afternoon
If time permits, walk along the ridge (► 154) from the café, then take the cable-car back down to ⭐Malcesine (► 78) and explore the town's narrow streets and castle.

Late Afternoon
From Mascéline continue north beside the lake, enjoying the views across the water to your left and of the flanks of ⭐Monte Baldo (► 81) to your right. Continue around Monte Brione to reach ⭐Riva del Garda (► 85).

Evening
The view of the lake from Monte Brione is exceptional so the short drive to the top is worthwhile. Or you could perhaps head north on the road to Trento for 6km (4mi) to reach **31** Arco (► 92). Alternatively, if walking on Monte Baldo has left you short of time or energy, just enjoy Riva's lakeside location before having a meal at one of the numerous restaurants in the town (► 94).

★2 Malcesine & Monte Baldo

The red and ochre-coloured buildings and *palazzi* in Malcesine are closely grouped around the castle and harbour. A stroll through the twisty lanes reveals lots of delightful hidden corners and shady squares with cafés, a number of boutiques and souvenir shops. The highest mountain on Lake Garda towers above the town – the majestic Monte Baldo massif stretches 35km (22mi) down the eastern side of the lake as far as Torri del Benaco in the south.

North of Peschiera del Garda the *Gardesana Orientale*, as the road beside the lake is called, runs through the **Riviera degli Olivi** (Olive Riviera). In its early stages the road passes more vines than olive trees, but further north the silvery leaves of the trees shimmer on the hillside, seemingly mirroring the light bouncing off the waves on the lake. Beyond Cassone is the Val di Sogno (Valley of Dreams) which is as peaceful as its name. Offshore here are two small islands, Isola Sogno and Isola dell'Olivo (of dreams and olives), while ahead is Malcesine, the highlight of the eastern side of the lake.

Malcesine's Castello Scaligero sits on top of a rocky outcrop that drops down to the lake below

Malcesine

The town is dominated by the **Castello Scaligero** dating from the 13th and 14th centuries. Much of the fortress is difficult to see unless you are on a boat. From the lake the genius of the construction is visible – a series of fortified walls surrounding three courtyards tumbling down a rugged headland. The whole complex is now a museum and open to the public. On the left, after passing through the main entrance, is the *casermetta* (small barracks) of 1620 which now houses two little natural history museums focussing on the flora, geology and

The whole fortress complex, comprising several different buildings, is now a museum and open to the public

birdworld of Monte Baldo (Museo del Baldo) and the flora and fauna of Lake Garda (Museo del Garda). The balcony at the other end of the courtyard offers views of the mountains. Stairs lead up to the former gunpowder magazine which now houses the 'Goethe Chamber'. A copy of a drawing the German writer made while at the castle during his 'Italian Journey' – and which almost landed him in prison (▶81, box) – is kept in the room. Another set of steps leads through a portal to a third courtyard with a cistern (water reservoir) and a fresco of the Virgin Mary in the Late Byzantine style. A fishing museum (Museo della Pesca) is on the ground floor of the main building. Apart from exhibits related to fishing

Eastern Lake Garda

there are pictures of Venetian warships being heaved over the mountains to Lake Garda in 1435 (Nago-Torbole, ► 92) and of attempts to salvage the man-of-war that sunk off Lazise (► 89). The upper storey and the tower can only be accessed by an external staircase. The masonry of the five-storey tower that was probably built by the Lombards, shows how far up the old tower reached (► 137). A window, now with bars, reveals where the drawbridge once was. From the platform at the top of the tower you can enjoy the famous view over the roofs of the town and across the lake.

The wide Corso Garibaldi leads right into the middle of the medieval **Old Town**. On the left is the **Piazza Statuto**, with the town hall on its eastern side. The lake and harbour lie just below the square. To the north there are lots of little alleys that open up into pretty squares with cafés, bars and shops. The castle, located higher up, is well signposted and reached via twisty little lanes. There is no lakeside prome-nade between the harbour and the castle but only side roads leading to the lake. Several cafés and restaurants however have terraces right on the water.

The crenelated Gothic **Palazzo dei Capitani** – which gen-erally served as the governor's residence on the eastern side of the lake – is a reminder of Venetian rule (1405–1797). The entrance leads through a vestibule with a huge ceiling fresco depicting the castle, into a pretty little garden right on the lakeside. The tourist information office is in the left wing. The assembly hall (Sala delle Sedute), with a long Renaissance frieze and a slightly smaller audience cham-ber – also with frescos – now used for a variety of events, is on the upper floor. A long promenade from the harbour leads southwards past several beaches to a green promon-tory (45 mins.), the **Val di Sogno** (Valley of Dreams). Tiny Isola dell'Olivo juts out of the water just off the Lido Sopri and, from the beach at the southern end of the promonto-ry, Isola del Sogno can be seen.

Anyone arriving in Malcesine by boat has the best view of the town located on the eastern side of the lake

The maze of little lanes in the Old Town of Malcesine leads to lots of little squares where cafés invite you to have a short break from shopping

Monte Baldo

From Malcesine a cable-car will take you to the top of Monte Baldo, either to enjoy the view or for a walk along the ridge (▶ 154). The flank of the great peak overlooking the lake is often known as the Botanical Garden of Italy because of the variety and profusion of plant species. Two parks have been set up to protect the plant and wildlife. The **Riserva Naturale Integrale Lostoni Selva Pezzi** has one boundary which follows the crest of Monte Baldo's ridge, the lower boundary running above the lakeside road. The second park, the **Riserva Naturale Integrale Gardesana Orientale**, is at the foot of the hill between Malcesine and Torbole.

The change in vegetation visible from the cable-car is marked. Close to the lake there are olive groves together with holm oak and Mediterranean pine. Higher up there are alpine species such as gentians, alpine orchids (including black vanilla, small white, toothed and spurred fragrant orchids) and plants such as *Lilium bulbiferum* and

---

A GERMAN WRITER – OR AN AUSTRIAN SPY

"On 3rd September [1786] at three in the morning, I slipped away from Carlsbad; one would not otherwise have let me go. It was quite obvious that I wanted to move on. I did not let that hinder me as it was high time!" Johann Wolfgang von Goethe wrote this entry in his diary at the start of his trip to Italy that lasted just under two years. He described this time in depth in his *Italian Journey* and later mentioned several times that this was the happiest time in his life. However, shortly after the beginning of his journey, it seemed as if things were not going to turn out so well. On 13 September he only escaped being arrested in Malcesine – near what was then the border between Venice and Austria – by a hair's breadth! He was seen sketching the castle that, for him, was nothing other than a 'ruinous pile of stones'. The Venetians on the other hand took him to be an Austrian spy, sent out to reconnoitre military installations. It was only with some effort that he managed to convince the suspicious locals that he was driven by an urge for knowledge rather than any political intentions.

Eastern Lake Garda

Cyclamen purpurascens or orange or tiger lily and purple cyclamen, while at the top of the ridge the species are those that would be expected on Arctic tundra rather than sun-soaked southern Europe – saxifrages and mountain avens, for example. As well as plants familiar from other European sites, Monte Baldo has three endemic plants, an anemone *(Anemone baldensis)*, a bedstraw *(Galium baldensis)* and a speedwell *(Veronica bonorata)*. North of Malcesine, the builders of the Gardesana Orientale had so little room between the lake and the mountainside that they had to resort to tunnelling. The shorter of the two tunnels crosses the regional border between Veneto and Trentino.

Monte Baldo offers a string of breathtakingly beautiful views of 'Benaco', as the lake is also called after Benacus, a Celtic deity once revered in Upper Italy

TAKING A BREAK

Insider Tip

In the town, **Caffè al Porto** and **Bar San Marco**, both situated on the small harbour, can be recommended. Even Goethe visited San Marco while touring Italy.

➕ 181 D4

Museo Castello Scaligero
☎ 045 6 57 03 33
🕑 April–Oct daily 9:30–7 💶 €6

Cable-car to Monte Baldo
🕑 Summer daily 8–5, winter 8–4. Every 30 mins., journey about 10 mins. The cable-car is usually closed in Nov and early Dec for maintenance work
💶 €10 (return: €15)

INSIDER INFO

■ The brave of heart who fancy a **tandem paraglide jump** from Monte Baldo have the opportunity to soak in the best views imaginable and enjoy the freedom of hovering high above the lake. The take-off point is at an altitude of 1800m (5905ft) and is open to anyone aged between 12 and 80 weighing between 40 and 110kg (88/245lb). No preparatory exercises or experience are needed. Flights last between 30 and 45 mins., landing on the lake near Malcesine (price: €100; www.paragliding-academy.com).

Insider Tip

■ Head for the small settlement of **Cassone** nearby and marvel at what must surely be **one of the shortest rivers in the world** – the **Aril** is just 175m (574ft) long and even has a little waterfall!

⭐ Garda

This popular holiday resort has a remarkably mild climate as it is sheltered from the wind between the slopes of Monte Luppia to the north and the table mountain in the south with the ruins of a medieval castle perched on top.

The remains of pile dwellings in the lake at the foot of the 'Rocca' and the ruins of a Celtic holy site on the mountain are evidence of the very early settlement of Garda. In the late 5th century, Theoderic the Great, King of the Ostrogoths, built a castle here. However, it was a woman in the 10th century who was to play a key role in the history of Garda and, in fact, of the whole of Italy. The Lombard Berengar II was living in the castle at this time and had his sights set on becoming king of Italy – but King Lothair II of Provence was in his way. It is highly likely that Berengar ordered him to be murdered and abducted Lothair's widow, Adelaide, in 951 and held her captive in the castle. Berengar was a tactical thinker. She should marry his son and strengthen his claim to the Italian throne. Adelaide refused and Berengar had her thrown into the dungeon. However, Adelaide managed to escape and became the wife of the Holy Roman Emperor Otto the Great who conquered Berengar and had him imprisoned for the rest of his life in Bamberg in Germany. Towards the end of the 13th century, Garda was ruled by the della Scala family; from the beginning of the 15th century it fell to Venice. Under Venetian rule the town blossomed but the castle was abandoned.

The air, the light, the blue of the southern sky and the vegetation became 'a daily delight', as Goethe wrote. And anyone pausing at the harbour on a mild summer's evening cannot really feel any differently to the poet.

The town and 'Rocca'

The beautiful *palazzi* in the Old Town were built in the 15th/16th centuries under the Venetians. The Venetian Gothic **Palazzo del Capitano** is prominently positioned on the harbour. The water once lapped the base of the pale

Eastern Lake Garda

yellow building with its six lancet windows before the harbour basin was filled in and the **Piazza Catullo** with its cafés and trattorias extended. The master architect Michele Sanmicheli of Verona built the **Palazzo Carlotti** (also known as the Palazzo Losa) on the harbour too. The arcade on the ground floor of this Renaissane building is crowned by a loggia with five arches.

The principal thoroughfare, **Corso V Emanuele**, runs parallel to the lakeside promenade and becomes Via S. Stefano further south and then Corso XX Settembre with gateways to the town at each end. The Palazzo Fregoso was built in 1510 near the north gate.

The most most important building in Garda is at the northern end of the Old Town behind a high wall. The yellow section of the **Villa Albertini** is the oldest part dating from 1779. The red towers with their ornamental battlements where added in the 19th century. The King of Sardinia and Piedmont, Carlo Alberto, stayed in the Villa Albertini in Garda on 10 June 1848 from where the annexation of Lombardy to his kingdom was proclaimed following a plebiscite. The villa is privately owned and not open to the public.

A walk to the ruins of the Rocca on the 300m-high hill to the southeast of the town takes just under an hour and offers a wonderful view of the lake. Sturdy shoes are recommended. Turn left next to the church of **Santa Maria Maggiore** (15th century, later remodelled in the Baroque style) into Via S. Bernardo that bends right after just a few yards. The Via degli Alpini will be seen on the right that then leads up the hill.

THE NYMPH WITH BLUE HAIR

According to legend, the town and the lake got their name from the blue-haired nymph, Engardina who stole the heart of a young water god. He made a big lake for her and, when she dived into it, the water turned the beautiful blue colour of her locks. As delightful as this tale may be, the name 'Garda' is most probably a corruption of the Alemanic *warden* meaning 'to observe' that, in turn, became *garden* – 'castle' in Old German.

TAKING A BREAK

The **Bar da Franco** on the lake can be recommended for a cup of coffee as can the **Trattoria Bar Bella Venezia** at Vicolo del Pio 12.

✚ 180 C2

INSIDER INFO

- There is a **good market** in the Old Town every Friday morning.
- A door to the right of the church of Santa Maria Maggiore leads to the **cloisters of a former monastery** from the 14th century. Stones with ornamental carvings dating from the Lombard era have been set in the wall above the stairs to the loggia.
- The **walk up to Rocca** that takes just under an hour is best in the morning light or in the early evening. Watching the sun go down from there is superb and the path down is straightforward by twilight.

⭐5 Riva del Garda

The elegant town that is one of the biggest and best-known holiday resorts in the area has one of the most important harbours on the lake as well as a beautiful Old Town. While many a beach on Lake Garda is no wider than a towel, the beach in Riva is so big that it is seldom jammed packed even in high season in August. There are lots of trees that provide shade and access to the beach is free of charge.

The *palazzi* built in the Lombard-Venetian style (the Palazzo Municipale can be seen on the right) and the arcades in Riva reflect the influence of both Verona and La Serenissima

Riva is on the northwest of Lake Garda and is flanked by two mountains. To the east it is separated from neighbouring Torbole by Monte Brione that is a mere 376m (1233ft) high. To the west, the rocky foothills of Monte Rocchetta (1521m/4990ft) rise steeply above the town. Its strategically favourable location that enabled it to take control of the trade route crossing the Alps on a north/south route and extending as far as the Po plain, made it much coveted – first by the Princely-Bishops of Trentino, then by the Counts of Arco, the Scaliger family from Verona, the Viscontis of Milan and the Venetians. The decisive maritime battle fought between the Venetians and the Milanese, that resulted in the Venetians gaining control of the whole of the Lake Garda region, took place off Riva in 1438. After the Congress of Vienna in 1815, Riva fell to Austria and remained under Austrian rule until 1918. Around 1900 the town was a popular destination for aristocrats and the upper class as well as for artists and writers. Franz Kafka, Thomas Mann, Friedrich Nietzsche, Rainer Maria Rilke, Sigmund Freud and D.H. Lawrence are just some of the famous who spent some time here.

The **Piazza Tre Novembre** on the harbour lies at the centre of the Old Town. Of all the brightly painted buildings with

Eastern Lake Garda

their long arcades, an ensemble of three grand *palazzi* on the west side – which now includes the town hall – stands out in particular. The **Palazzo Pretorio** and the **Palazzo del Provveditore** on a corner site both date from the 14th century and were built by Cansignorio della Scala. The **Palazzo Municipale** where the Venetian governor resided was added in the 15th century. An arcade and a castelated town gateway (Porta Bruciata) lead to the little **Piazza Rocco**. The open apse of the former church of San Rocco can be seen on the right. On the eastern side of the square is the slightly leaning 34m (112ft)-high **Torre Apponale** which was built as a fortification and integrated in the town wall in the 13th century. The Rocca to the east of the Torre Apponale is surrounded by green on a little island with a moat. It was erected by the Scaligers in 1124 and later remodelled by the Austrians who used it as a barracks. It houses the **Museo Alto Garda** with its display of archaeological finds

Friedrich Nietzsche was so taken by the leaning clock tower, the Torre Apponale, on the eastern side of the Piazza Rocco on the harbour front, that he said that he would like to live there as a hermit at the end of his life

INSIDER INFO

One of two exquisitely beautiful ships, the **paddle steamer 'Zanardelli'** that dates from 1903, operates exclusively in the north around Riva, Limone, Malcesine and Torbole. The fastest **direct link** between **Riva and Peschiera,** i.e. the longest stretch, takes 3.5 hours. A **round trip of the whole lake** taking in all the most important places can only be done in one day if you go without visiting the individual places en route. The section Riva – Malcesine costs €7.50; timetable: www.navigazionelaghi.it.

from the region and a collection of paintings from the 16th to the 20th centuries.

Surrounding area
From Riva take the 421 – towards Lago di Tenno – for 4km (2mi) to reach Varone where a waterfall plunges 90m (294ft) into a narrow gorge. Walkways have been constructed to allow you to get close to the 🏞️**Cascata del Varone** and admire their power and experience the noise and spray. Waterproof clothing is recommended.

TAKING A BREAK

Riva has one of the most beautiful promenades on the lake. Sit at a table here, at **Caffè Città**, for example, or at a restaurant on the Piazza Tre Novembre to enjoy it at its best. There are also plenty of alternatives in the town centre for a break – try the **Maroni pasticceria** on the corner of Via Maria and Piazza Cavour.

Insider Tip

➕ 181 D5

Museo Alto Garda (MAG) & Torre Apponale (Rocca di RivaTorre)
☎ 04 64 57 38 69; www.museoaltogarda.it
🕐 March–2 Nov Tue–Sun 10–6; June, July, Aug, Sep daily
💶 Museum and tower individually, each costing €2, combined ticket €3

Cascata del Varone
☎ 04 64 52 14 21
🕐 May–Aug daily 9–7; April, Sep 9–6; March, Oct 9–5, Nov–Feb Sun and public holidays only 10–5
💶 €5.50

INSIDER INFO

- A stroll around the Old Town should also include a visit to the 'Church of the Holy Virgin', Riva's most important art-historical building. Built in the early 17th century by an unknown Portuguese architect, the **Chiesa dell'Inviolata** has an elaborate Baroque, octagonal interior – all gilding and plasterwork.
- Some 200m above the town, a round tower sticks out above the treetops on the slopes of **Monte Rocchetta**. It is the last remnant of a Venetian fortress destroyed by the French in 1703. It offers wonderful views over the town and the lake.
- A lovely promenade along the shore takes you as far as **Monte Brione**, past mile-long beaches and well-looked after lawned areas for sunbathing, as well as bars and campsites.
- If you are particularly interested in **lake dwellings**, go the museum at Lake Ledro (►62) rather than the one here in the Rocca.

At Your Leisure

22 San Martino della Battaglia & Solferino

A visit to San Martino, Solferino and Castiglione delle Stiviere to the south of Desenzano brings you face to face with the 'Risorgimento', the struggle for Italian unification against the Austrian Empire and the Habsburgs and the decisive Battle of Solferino that was fought on 24 June 1859. The appalling suffering by thousands of wounded soldiers, left to die an agonising death on the battlefield without medical help, led to the founding of the Red Cross by the Swiss humanist and devout Christian Henri Dunant. On a clear day, the 65m (213ft)-high tower at San Martino – which was given the epithet 'della Battaglia' – can be seen from Lake Garda. A 400m-long ramp spirals upwards culminating in a viewing platform. The walls on the ramp are covered in paintings of the Italian war of independence. The Museo della Battaglia just a few yards beyond the tower has displays of uniforms, equipment, shredded flags, letters and coins from the war in 1859. The *ossario* houses more than 1400 skulls and the skeletal remains of fallen soldiers.

Riva
del Garda
31
30
Malcesine
& Monte
Baldo
29 Garda
28
27
26
22 24 25
22 23

➕ 180 B1

Torre di San Martino e Museo
☎ 030 9 91 03 70
🕐 March–Sep daily 9–12:30, 2:30–7,
Oct–Feb Tue–Sun 9–12:30, 2–4:30
🎟 €2.50

Museo Della Croce Rossa
✉ Via Garibaldi 50,
46044 Castiglione delle Stiviere
☎ 03 76 63 85 05
🕐 April–Oct Tue–Sun 9–noon, 3–6,
Nov–Feb 9–noon, 2–5
🎟 €5

23 Parco Giardino Sigurta

About 8km (5mi) south of Peschiera, near Valeggio sul Mincio, is the 60ha (148 acre) Parco Giardino Sigurtà, the work of Count Carlo Sigurtà (1898–1983). Using water from the River Mincio, for which the count had secured the rights, he transformed the dry, hilly, moraine landscape into one of the most beautiful landscaped gardens in Europe. Sigurtà devoted himself to tending the park for almost 40 years; it was then taken over by his nephew, Enzo. The park has been open to the public since 1978.
➕ 180 C1   ☎ 045 6 37 10 33
🕐 April–Sep daily 9–7; Oct–Nov 9–6
🎟 €12

24 Peschiera del Garda

Peschiera, where the River Mincio leads out of Lake Garda, has always been strategically important. It was occupied by the Romans and, in medieval times, there was a castle and a walled harbour. When the Austrians held the area they demolished the castle but reinforced the walls, making Peschiera one corner of their defensive quadrilateral, the other corners being Legnago, Mantova and Verona. The

The church of Madonna del Frassino to the south of Peschiera attracts lots of pilgrims

Austrian defences remain and are still uncompromising, although overgrown. They can best be seen from a boat.

In the main square look for the town hall clock with the beaks of two bronze eagles striking the hour.

➕ 180 C1

🎡 Gardaland

Gardaland, just north of Peschiera, is Italy's biggest and most popular theme park. New features are added each year so that those who keep coming back time and again will not get bored at all. It is safe to say that if you have children and they like roller-coasters, water rides, fantasy characters, dolphins, safaris, play areas and much, much more, they will love Gardaland. The park caters for children from 'just walking' upwards and there are plenty of refreshments. Sealife and the Delfinarium also belong to Gardaland. At weekends in summer a free shuttle bus runs from the station in Peschiera to Gardaland. At this time of year, both the park

and the car parks in particular are generally full to bursting.

➕ 180 C2 ☎ 045 6 44 97 77

🕐 Easter–June and last two weeks of Sept daily 10–6; July to mid-Sept 9–midnight, Oct Sat–Sun 9:30–6

💶 €31. Entrance is free for carers of disabled visitors and children under m (3ft) tall. There is a reduced entry fee for under 10s and over 60s.

🏰 Lazise

An intact town wall surrounds the historical centre of Lazise. As this is a traffic-free zone you can stroll around the pretty medieval lanes with their shops, cafés, *trattorias* and restaurants at your leisure. In the Middle Ages the Roman settlement of Lasitium rose to become a market town with a castle. The Scaligers rebuilt the fortress in the 13th century and gave it the appearance it still has today with castellated towers and a walkway along the battlements. Under Venetian rule it became a place of key importance. Today, the Scaliger castle is lived in and, together with the Villa Bernini, surrounded by a park (not open to the public). The narrow harbour basin at the end of the Piazza Vittorio Emanuele is surrounded by a row of pretty houses with restaurants and *trattorias*. The two wide arches of the Arsenal (Vecchia Dogana) from the 14th century open towards both the harbour and the lake. The building of random white stone and pebbles served as a customs house, among other things. Today, it is used for temporary exhibitions. The slender belltower of the church of San Nicolò (12th century), which is decorated with beautiful frescos, rises behind the Arsenal.

➕ 180 D2

27 Bardolino

Among the best known winegrowing areas around the shores of the lake is the region around Bardolino where the red wine of the same name is pressed. There is a **museum of wine** in the town and you can follow a route through the wine growing area (➤ 165). But Bardolino does not turn its back on olives and one of the exhibits at the the **Museo dell'Olio d'Oliva** is a hydraulically driven olive press from the 19th century.

The Piazza Matteotti – actually more a wide promenade than a square – with its many shops, cafés and *trattorias*, forms the heart of the Old Town. The entrance to the Neo-Classicistic church of **Santi Nicolò e Severo** is flanked by four tall columns (19th century). Open-air concerts given by the Bardolino Philharmonic Orchestra are held between June and September every Wednesday evening with the church as a backdrop.

A delapidated tower on the lakeside promenade is all that remains of the Scaliger fortress. Lovely walks are to be had from the lakeside promenade: to the north as far as Garda (3km/1.8mi), passing olive groves, bathing areas and small clumps of trees en route and, to

the south to Cisano. **San Severo**, with its tall slender *campanile*, is one of the most beautiful and best preserved Romanesque churches in the area around Verona. The layout of the random stone building that dates from the end of the 11th century is not symmetrical – the length and width of the side aisles are different. Inside, the walls are covered with unusually vibrant frescos. One of the oldest buildings from the Carolingian period is the small church of **San Zeno**, tucked away in the Via San Zeno. The tiny, narrow single-aisled building that seems unusually high was constructed in the 8th century to a cruciform plan. At the end of the Borgo Cavour is the grand, privately-owned villa of the local, long-established Guerrieri Rizzardi family. It lies in a large park laid out in the 16th century that stretches down to the lakeside promenade. Wine and oil produced on the estate is sold in a shop next to the gate.

➕ 180 D2

Museo del Vino
✉ Via Costabella 9 ☎ 045 6 22 83 31; www.museum.it 🕐 8:30–12:30, 2:30–6:30, except on public holidays in Dec and Jan 🎟 Free

Museo dell'Olio d'Oliva
✉ Via Peschiera 54 ☎ 045 6 22 90 47 🕐 Mar to mid-Jan 9–12:30, 2:30–7 🎟 Free

28 Punta di San Vigilio
The Romans were obviously captivated by the charm of this

Punta di San Vigilio: this little promontory is one of the most beautiful spots on Lake Garda

promontory covered in meadows, olive groves and cypress tree that lies 3km (1.8mi) to the west of Garda, as they built a villa here. The privately-owned **Villa Guarienti** now occupies the site at the end of an avenue of cypresses. Laurence Olivier and Winston Churchill stayed in the luxurious hotel Locanda di San Vigilio which has just 14 rooms. A church dedicated to a 13th-century hermit, San Vigilio, a private marina and a restaurant are also located here. Anyone wanting to swim around the Punta may do so from the spotless **Baia delle Sirene** (Bay of the Sirens) which also boasts a restaurant, showers and a children's play area.

➕ 180 C2

Public bathing area

✉ Parco Baia delle Sirene
🕐 Mon–Sat 9:30am–8pm, Sun 9am–8pm
💶 €12

29 Torri del Benaco

Another Scaligeri castle, still attached to a section of the Old Town walls, guards the headland that overlooks the eastern terminus of Lake Garda's only car ferry. The imposing castle is now a museum documenting industries from local olive oil and lemon production to lake fishing and quarrying – Torri

Eastern Lake Garda

del Benaco was once well-known for its reddish-yellow marble, used for many buildings in Verona, for example.

There is also a collection of pre-historic rock engravings from the area. The old lemon-trading house, **Lemonaia**, built in 1760, can also be visited: the building is one of few that now survive from the time when lemons were as important as olives to the economy around Lake Garda.

The church of **Santa Trinità** with 14th-century frescoes in the style of Giotto is well worth a visit. The *chiesa* is situated on the pretty, old harbour at the heart of Torri del Benaco, overlooked by the castle built to protect it.

✚ 180 C3

Museo del Castello Scaligero di Torri del Benaco and Lemonaia
☎ 045 6 29 61 11 🕐 June–Sep daily 9:30–1, 4:30–7:30; April–May and Oct 9:30–12:30, 2:30–6 💶 €4

🗓 Nago-Torbole

While, generally speaking, only a few tourists a year find their way to Nago, a village located some 150m (492ft) up on a rocky plateau above the local centre, Torbole, thousands stream to the beach below. Torbole sits snugly on the shore of the lake and has become one of the most important centres for surfing and sailing on Lake

Garda. Mountainbikers and climbers find ideal conditions here too as the north of Lake Garda is almost entirely enclosed by mountains with well signposted hiking trails and climbing routes. The only noteworthy sight in Nago is the ruined fort (13th century), first mentioned in 1210, that once guarded the Val d'Adige area down to Lake Garda. The strategically sited fort was owned in turn by the Counts of Arco, the Castelbarco family, the province of Trentino and the Venetians, before it was slighted by the French in 1703.

✚ 181 D5

🗓 Arco

To the north of Lake Garda, some 6km (3.7mi) from Riva and Nago-Torbole, is the steep-side Arco mountain with its castle. At its foot is the pristine climatic health resort with avenues of palm trees, beautifully renovated Renaissance buildings and pretty shops. The mild climate of this little town was the reason why the Habsburg Archduke Albrecht of Austria chose to move to his winter residence here from 1872 onwards. Nowadays Arco attracts freeclimbers in particular. Every year in September the 'Rock Master' world championships are held in Arco. The arboretum in Arco (**Arboreto**), originally the park surrounding the archducal palace, has miniature landscaped areas focussing on the native countries of various plants.

✚ 181 D5

Castello di Arco
✉ Via Castello
☎ 04 64 51 01 56
🕐 April–Sep daily 10–7; Oct–Feb 10–4
💶 €4

Parco Arciducale Arboreto
✉ Via Lomego
☎ 04 64 58 36 36
🕐 April–Sep 8–7; Oct–March 94
💶 Free

Where to...
Stay

Prices

Expect to pay per double room, per night

€ under €80   €€ €80–€130   €€€ over €130

BARDOLINO

Aqualux €€

One of the best spa hotels on the lake with six pools and six saunas, located on the outskirts of the town.

⊞ 180 D2 ⊠ Via Europa Unita 24
☎ 045 6 22 99 99; www.aqualuxhotel.com

Hotel du Lac et Bellevue €€€

90 rooms and suites, restaurant, bar, pool, sauna, gym and jetty in a peaceful situation.

⊞ 180 C2 ⊠ Via Santa Cristina ☎ 045 6 21 03 55; www.hotel-du-lac-et-bellevue-bardolino.it

GARDA

Locanda San Vigilio €€€

In an exquisite position on Punta San Vigilio; superbly furnished bedrooms, a private harbour, a sun terrace and much more; expensive.

⊞ 180 C2 ⊠ Punta San Vigilio
☎ 045 7 25 66 88; www.punta-sanvigilio.it

LAZISE

Principe di Lazise €€

Pretty country hotel on the edge of the town in a hilly area rather like Tuscany. Pool and very good spa facilities and restaurant.

⊞ 180 D2 ⊠ Località La Greghe ☎ 045 6 49 01 77; www.hotelprincipedilazise.com

MALCESINE

Hotel Aurora €   Insider Tip

One of the most romantically sited hotels with contemporary furnishings on the eastern shore, at the heart of Malcesine. Facilities are limited – although there is parking – but the rooms are comfortable.

⊞ 181 C4 ⊠ Piazza Vittorio Emanuele
☎ 045 7 40 01 14; www.aurora-malcesine.com

👫 Villa Monica €€

Located on one of the most beautiful beaches on the lake to the north of the town. Indoor swimming pool, car park.

⊞ 181 C4 ⊠ Località Baitone
☎ 045 6 57 01 11; www.villamonica.com

PESCHIERA DEL GARDA

Hotel Ristorante Bel Sito €

Ideally positioned for excursions to local attractions and Verona. Swimming pool, garden and tennis court; bike hire available.

⊞ 180 C1 ⊠ Via Venezia 62
☎ 045 6 40 09 21; www.belsitohotel.com

RIVA DEL GARDA

Lido Palace €€€

This most-recently opened 5-star hotel is a perfect blend of traditional and contemporary styles and one of the best hotels on the lake. Very good restaurant, very elegant spa.

⊞ 181 D5 ⊠ Via Carducci 10
☎ 04 64 02 18 99; www.lido-palace.it

TORRI DEL BENACO

Baia dei Pini €€€

The villa is right on the beach, furnished in a modern but rather idiosyncratic style. 3-star but feels like 4; pool and car park.

⊞ 180 C3 ⊠ Via Gardesana 115
☎ 045 7 22 52 15; www.baiadeipini.com

Where to...
Eat and Drink

Prices
Expect to pay for a three-course meal for one, excluding drinks and service
€ under €30   € €30–€60   €€€ over €60

BARDOLINO

Café Italia €€
This is more a wine bar than a café, with a good selection of local wines to complement fresh dishes.
➕ 180 D2 ✉ Piazza Principe Amadeo 2–4
☎ 045 7 21 15 85 🕐 Closed Tue March–Oct and Mon–Fri Nov–Feb

BRENZONE

Belvedere €
This family-run restaurant offers regional specialities such as rabbit, homemade noodles and pizza baked in a wood-fired oven. Excellent selection of *grappa*.
➕ 180 D4 ✉ Località Marniga
☎ 045 7 42 00 55 🕐 Closed Tue

GARDA

Bussola Domani €
The owner makes the pasta and there is a choice of fish or meat for a main course. There is a garden at the back for *al fresco* dining.
➕ 180 C2 ✉ Via Spagna 29
☎ 045 7 25 64 75 🕐 Closed Nov–March

 **Insider Tip**
Trattoria Al Graspo €€€
'I am the menu', says the chef and owner, Luca. Lots of meat; good fish.
➕ 180 C2 ✉ Piazza Calderini 12
☎ 045 7 25 60 46 🕐 Closed Nov–March

LAZISE

Alla Grotta €€
On the old harbour across from the Venetian Customs House and the old church. Inside, the large open fire is used, in part, for cooking. Traditional Italian fare.
➕ 180 D2 ✉ Via F. Fontana 8
☎ 045 7 58 00 35 🕐 Closed Tue

Corte Olivo €€
In the summer the tables are in a lovely inner courtyard inside the Old Town walls. Traditional menu.
➕ 180 D2 ✉ Corso Cangrande 22
☎ 045 7 58 13 47 🕐 Closed Tue

MALCESINE

Vecchia Malcesine €€€
The menu is extensive and includes fish from the lake (try the poached pike), seafood and meat dishes, as well as traditional fare with a twist. Extensive wine list; booking advised.
➕ 181 C4 ✉ Via Pisort 6
☎ 045 7 40 04 69 🕐 Closed Wed, Feb and lunch Nov–Jan and March

PESCHIERA DEL GARDA

La Torretta €€
Eat in a fine old building with wooden beams in the heart of old Peschiera – or sit outside under the sun umbrellas.
➕ 180 C1 ✉ Via G Galilei 12
☎ 045 7 55 01 08 🕐 Closed Wed

RIVA DEL GARDA

Mediterraneo €€
Pleasant restaurant serving traditional Italian meals and pizzas cooked in a charcoal stove.
➕ 181 D5 ✉ Piazza Garibaldi 6
☎ 04 64 55 01 75 🕐 Closed Tue

Where to...
Shop

BARDOLINO

Augusta at Piazza Matteotti 37–39 has a big choice of women's shoes, bags and clothes. For something different try the studio of **Maura Bontempi** on the Piazza Statuto. *Insider Tip*

GARDA

For leather goods go to **Mola** (Corso Vittorio Emanuele 40). Beautiful jewellery can be found at **Modini** (Corso Vittorio Emanuele 26) and at **Bella e Buona** (no. 38) there is a tempting range of gifts.

For art, **Garda Ceramiche** (Via A. Manzoni 20) has excellent ceramics whereas **Studio per l'Arte** (Calle dei Sottoportici 6) is run by Adriano Foschi, an eclectic painter who also sells art material.

LAZISE

For ceramics, try **Il Gatto Nero** (Corso Ospedale 33). **Antico Mulino alla Torre** (Via Raffaello 35) stocks Italian crafts, jewellery, soaps and basketware, while **Clacson** (Corso Ospedale 28) has lovely children's clothes.

MALCESINE

Millenium Pelletteria (Piazza Statuto 18) has a good selection of handbags and other leatherware. For jewellery try **Voglia d'Oro** (Via Capitanato 1). There are few art outlets in town. The best is **Onice** (Corso Garibaldi 53) which specialises in ceramics.

For a good selection of lace, candles, oils and gifts head for **Casanova (Vicolo di Mezzo 5).**

PESCHIERA DEL GARDA

It is worth having a peek in **Più Gioielli** (Via Rocca 21) for jewellery and silverware, **Antichità** (Via Cavallotti) opposite the tourist information office, for antiques and **Candela d'Arte Giesse** (Piazza Betteloni 14), next to the tourist office, for handmade candles.

RIVA DEL GARDA

For something different try **Fronte Lago** (Viale San Francesco 9) which has weird but wonderful bags and scarves.

For jewellery head for **Easy Gold** (Via Santa Maria 3), **Orafo** (Via Monatanara 16) that specialises in gold, or **Re Artu Bijoux** (Via Lipella) which has ultramodern jewellery.

TORBOLE

Coast to Coast (Via Lungolago Verona) is good for young fashion items; **Gioielleria Santoni** (also in Via Lungolago Verona) has lovely jewellery.

Surfing equipment and accessories are very much in demand. The legendary **Point-7 Store Torbole** is a little way out of town at Via Sabbioni 15 and always has the very latest for the surfing scene.

MARKETS

Bardolino – Monday, **Garda** – Friday, **Lazise** – Saturday, **Malcesine** – Saturday, **Peschiera del Garda** – Monday, **Riva del Garda** – 2nd and 4th Wednesdays of the month (June to September), 2nd Wednesday only from October to May, **Torbole** – 2nd and 4th Tuesday of the month, **Torri del Benaco** – Monday.

Antiques markets in **Bardolino** on every 3rd Sunday and, in **Torri del Benaco**, on Wednesdays in summer.

Where to...
Go Out

SPORT AND LEISURE

Watersports

There is a large number of wind-surfing and sailing schools at the northern end of the lake. For wind-surfing, the best schools are **Sailing du Lac** (at Hotel du Lac, tel: 04 64 55 24 53) in Riva del Garda and **Circolo Surf** (tel: 04 64 50 53 85), **Conca d'Oro Windsurf** (tel: 04 64 54 81 92), **Surfcenter Lido Blu** (at Hotel Lido Blu, tel: 04 64 50 63 49) and **Surf Segnana** (at Hotel Paradiso, tel: 04 64 50 59 63) in Torbole.

The **Stickl Sportcamp** is run by the former surfing world champion, Heinz Stickl (Via Gardesana 144 in Val di Sogno di Malcesine, tel: 045 7 40 16 97; www.stickl.com).

For sailing contact **Fraglia Vela Riva** (tel: 04 64 55 24 60), **Sailing Club Riva** (04 64 55 24 53), **Lega Navale Italiana** (tel: 04 64 55 52 01) or **Gardaseecharter** (tel: 33 55 27 45 54) in Riva del Garda, or **Circolo Vela Torbole** (tel: 04 64 50 62 40) and **Surf Segnana** (tel: 04 64 50 59 63) in Torbole.

There is a diving school at Riva del Garda – **Gruppo Sommozzatori**, at Porto S Nicolò (tel: 04 64 55 51 20).

Canoe tuition/hire is available from **Canoa Club Canottieri Riva** (tel: 04 64 55 52 94).

Adventure Sports

Several organisations for rock climb-ing, canyoning and paragliding are available in Riva del Garda, Torbole and Arco, at the northern end of the lake. A list is available from the local tourist offices.

For canyoning, contact **Canyon Adventures** (tel: 33 48 69 86 66) in Torbole.

Golf

The 18-hole **Club Paradiso del Garda** at Peschiera del Garda (tel: 03 65 91 35 40) is the only course on the eastern shore.

FESTIVALS

There is a **festival of medieval games** in Lazise in June.

Wine festivals are held in June in Peschiera and Bardolino. Peschiera also has a *palio* in August in which boats with single or double pairs of oars race along the town's canals.

The **Young Musicians' Festival** is held annually at the end of July in Riva del Garda.

Malcesine has a series of **music evenings** (8:30–10pm) during the summer – on the Piazza Cavour on Mondays, on the Piazza del Porto on Tuesdays, Thursdays and Sundays, and on the Piazza Matteotti on Fridays.

NIGHTLIFE

Of the towns on the eastern and northern sides of Lake Garda, Riva is the most lively place to go in the evenings. You can dance at the **Novecento** (Via Gazzoletti) and **No Name** (Piazza Catena).

If it's a pub or bar with music you want to visit for an evening out then try **Pub all'Oca** (Via Santa Maria 9), **Pub House** (Viale Rovereto 11), **Pub Lochness** (Viale Dante) and the **Barracuda** (Via dei Fabbri 11).

The only real disco in town is **Maracaibo** (Via Monte Oro 14). There is a better selection of discos in Arco located back from the lake. The ultimate hotspot for surfing gossip is in Torbole, at **Wind's Bar** (Via Matteotti 11) and the **Cutty Sark Pub** (Via Pontalti 2).

Summer evenings are always loud, long and lively at the **Beach Bar Vaca Loca** (Via Gardesana 9) in Assenza di Brenzone.

Verona

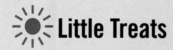 **Little Treats**

Alimentari out of a picture book

The sight and smell of the food in the **Antica Salumeria Albertini**, Corso Sant'Anastasia 41 makes you feel you are in a paradise for all the senses. Simply unbeatable!

Sweet kisses from Juliet

The **Pasticceria de Rossi** entices customers with 'Baci di Giulietta' (Juliet's Kisses) – sugar-coated marzipan. Give them a try: Corso Porta Borsari 3.

Nodi di Amore (Love Knots)

Tortellini – known as 'love knots' – were allegedly invented in Valeggio sul Mincio, an enchanting little town to the east of Verona. And they also taste best here too (www.ristorantivaleggio.it).

Getting Your Bearings

"It was the nightingale and not the lark / That pierced the fearful hollow of thine ear". With these lines Juliet tries to delay her Romeo's departure – and how the tale ends is world famous. Verona is also world famous for its open-air opera festival that takes place every year in July and August in the Arena, the third largest Roman amphitheatre still in existence in Italy. Located on the banks of the Adige with a historical centre that is listed as a UNESCO World Heritage Site, the city has a lot of other things to offer too.

To get an idea of the layout of the city, a wonderful view is to be had from the top of the Torre dei Lamberti. Verona, the capital of the province of the same name, is located on a bend in the River Adige, with ten bridges linking it to districts on the other bank. It was already an important site under the Romans from 89BC onwards. In the 6th century Theoderic the Great, King of the Ostrogoths (†526), made the city a royal seat alongside Pavia and Ravenna. Pippin (777–810), Charlemagne's second son, later held sway here as King of the Franks ruling over Italy. In the Middle Ages the German emperors chose the city at the end of the route over the Brenner Pass as the base for overseeing Upper Italy. In 1164 Verona entered a military alliance with other cities in eastern Upper Italy that was expanded in 1167 into the Lombard League. As a result of trading Verona became a city of considerable importance and was able to expand the extent of its rule. From the mid 13th century it was ruled by the princely house of della Scala (also written as Scaligeri or Scaliger) under whose governance the city reached the peak of its power. In 1387 Verona fell first to the Viscontis of Milan and, in 1405, to the Republic of Venice. In 1797 Verona and Venetia became Austrian and, together with Peschiera, Mantua and Legnago, formed a quadrilateral stronghold from 1814 onwards. When Austria lost Venetia to Italy the city was incorporated into the Kingdom of Italy in 1866.

Modern Juliets and a Romeo in Roman costume on the Piazza Bra

Getting Your Bearings

TOP 10

Don't Miss

At Your Leisure

The Perfect Day

At least one whole day should be devoted to exploring Verona. If you follow our suggested tour you will not miss any of the highlights. For more information see the main entries (➤ 102–118).

🕙 10:00

Having had breakfast head for the **39 Duomo Santa Maria Matricolare** (➤ 117). This is your first stop, after admiring the architecture of the building, consecrated in 1187, go inside to marvel at the works of art, looking especially for Titian's masterpiece, the *Assumption of the Virgin*, completed in 1532 (in the first chapel in the left-hand side aisle).

From the cathedral take Via Duomo southeast, following it past the **Galleria d'Arte Moderna**, to your right, to reach the huge **38 church of Sant'Anastasia** (➤ 116) with its Late Gothic frescos. Step inside to admire the works, particularly the Pisanello.

🕚 11:00

Continue along Via Duomo, then turn right into Via delle Arche Scaligere, soon passing the Casa di Romeo. This austere 14th-century house is known to have belonged to the Montecchi family, which Shakespeare anglicised to Montague, and has become, inevitably, Romeo's house. Continue to **37 Santa Maria Antica** (➤ 116) and then go through the arch to reach the ⭐**Piazza dei Signori** (➤ 108).

🕚 11:45

Having paid your respects to Dante (➤ 109) and admired the buildings that surround his statue on the Piazza dei Signori, climb the **Torre dei Lamberti** for a view over the square and the whole city.

🕧 12:30

The Piazza dei Signori (above) is linked to the ⭐**Piazza Erbe** (➤ 111) by the **Arco della Costa**, the 'arch of the rib'. The rib in question is a whale-bone suspended beneath the arch. Legend has it that it will fall on the first honest man who walks beneath it.

A variety of things are sold from stands around about including carnival masks. Soak in the atmosphere and leave the square in the southeast corner along Via Cappello, before turning left. Soon you will reach the **36 Casa di Giulietta** (➤ 115), with its evocative balcony, on the left.

🕜 1:30

From the Casa di Giulietta continue along Via Cappello, then turn first right along Via Stella, following it to the ⭐**Piazza Bra** (➤ 102). If you haven't already eaten, choose one of the pavement cafés/restaurants for lunch – perhaps **Liston** at no. 19 or the restaurant **Olivo** at no. 18a – admiring the outside of the Arena and, probably, a number of street artists.

🕝 2:45

Visit the **Arena** (➤ 104). A visit takes about an hour. Afterwards, walk back along Listone, then turn right along Via Roma to reach the **33 Castelvecchio** and **Ponte Scaligero** (➤ 114).

🕟 4:45

Reverse your route to Listone and have a cup of coffee at the **Café Opera** (no. 107). The crowds thin at this time of day so you will be able to relax and think about visiting the stalls on the Piazza delle Erbe before they close or shopping on Via Mazzini before having dinner.

⭐6 Piazza Bra & Arena di Verona

It's best to start a tour of the city at the Piazza Bra which, with the Arena di Verona in the middle, is one of the most visited squares.

Piazza Bra

The *piazza* is entered from the south through the Portoni della Bra, a twin-arched gateway with a tower that was added around 1400 by the Viscontis. *Palazzi* with frescos, arched windows and pretty balconies (16th–18th century) enclose the square which is lined with cafés and restaurants. The south side is marked by the **Gran Guardia Nuova (Palazzo Municipale)**, the city hall built between 1835 and 1843 with a semi-circular extension added after 1945. Next to this is the elongated former Gran Guardia, a Venetian building with a huge loggia (1614).

In the evening on the Piazza Bra: people strolling around the Arena and along the wide paved area

"AND THE STARS SHONE…"

A production of Verdi's *Aida* involves more than 700 people, from handworkers, technicians and lighting engineeers to scene-shifters, wardrobe attendants and production managers. The opera festival in the Arena is not a cheap undertaking – and it's not cheap for music lovers either. But what are materialistic thoughts compared to such a wonderful and unique evening in a historical setting under the stars? Or when nature and art merge into one and the painter Mario Cavaradossi launches into "And the stars shone" in the third act of Puccini's *Tosca*?

Stage sets and props are stored behind the Arena

Music instead of fights

The Roman amphitheatre was built at the time of the Flavian emperors (1st century). The Arena is a theatre of perfect proportions and its size is testimony to Verona's historical importance.

Verdi's *Aida* during the opera festival in the Arena

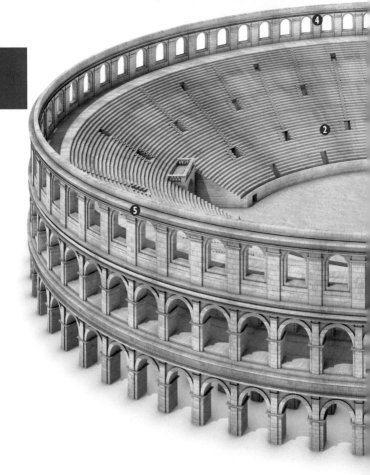

❶ Oval: The actual arena is a hollowed-out oval at the centre of the round building. This was where gladiator and bull fights as well as animal baiting took place. It measures almost 74m (242ft) long and 45m (148ft) wide.

❷ Cavea: The spectator area, known as the *cavea*, is made of tiered stones each 45cm (18in) high. Today, this area provides seating for up to 15,000 people. The overall external length of the elliptical plan, measured from the main entrance, is nearly 140m (455ft).

❸ Basement: Technical equipment now occupies the basement area of the amphitheatre. This was where

there were orginally rooms for the gladiators and cages for the animals.

❹ Velaria: The spectator area can be roofed over by a complex arrangement of awnings.

❺ Ala: The outer façade of the Arena *(ala)* was originally clad in stone. This was almost completely destroyed in an earthquake in 1183. Only one section at the northern end has survived and reveals the building's original height.

❻ Façade: The arches along the present façade were originally part of the building's interior. As can be seen, the reddish marble has been effected by exposure to the elements.

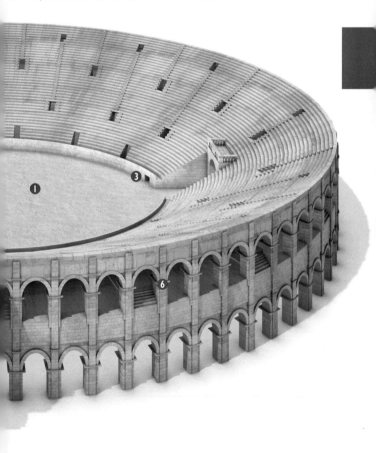

The Teatro Filarmonico concert hall (1716) and the **Museo Lapidario Maffeiano** are behind this. The scholar Scipione Maffei (1675–1755) of Verona had the latter built for his collection of Ancient Greek and Roman sculptures, sarcophagi, reliefs and much more.

Arena di Verona

The two-storey row of arcades that gives us the picture we have today of the Roman amphitheatre, built in the 1st century AD for gladiator and bull fights, was originally surrounded by another, three-storey outer wall of red Veronese marble. Only four arcades of the once magnificent façade now remain on the north side. The interior comprises an eliptical area (138m × 109m/453ft × 358ft) with 45 tiers and seating for 15,000. The Arena was damaged by earthquakes in the 12th and 13th centuries and, for a time, its stone was used for other buildings. It also served as a fortress and even as a place executions were held under the Scaliger. Its age-old walls were also the setting for medieval tournaments before craftsmen and prostitutes set themselves up in the arcades on the lower level. In 1913, to mark the 100th anniversary of Giuseppe Verdi's birth, an opera festival was held in the Arena for the first time. This now takes place every year between June and September.

TAKING A BREAK

The **Café Opera** at no. 10c is excellent for coffee while the **Olivo** at no. 18 is good for lunch.

➕ 183 D3

left: Waiters awaiting – how about an aperitif before an evening stroll?

Museo Lapidarium Maffeiano
☎ 045 59 00 87 🕐 Tue–Sun 8:30–1:30 💶 €6

Arena
☎ 045 8 00 32 04; www.arena.it
🕐 Mon 1:30–7:30, Tue–Sun 8:30–7:30. During the opera season the Arena closes at 2pm 💶 €7

INSIDER INFO

■ As well as being one of the best places in Verona for people-watching, the wide paved area (Liston) around the Piazza Bra, created in 1730, is the venue of choice for some of the city's best **street artists**. For good entertainment, have a few euros ready, buy a cup of coffee and wait.

■ The **Piazzetta Mura Gallieno**, rather like a courtyard behind the amphitheatre, is used for storing props for the various different operas performed during the festival season. On change-over days, cranes are used to heave the huge stage sets into or out of the Arena. You may even see the Sphinx fly...

■ In the **Museo Lapidarium Maffeiano**, find your way to the Roman funeral reliefs, which are among the best and certainly the most moving of the engraved stones.

Insider Tip

★7 Piazza dei Signori

The Piazza dei Signori, once Verona's administrative district and the seat of the government, is the city's elegant 'drawing room' surrounded by magnificent town palaces. Five large, richly decorated arches span the points where neighbouring streets join the square and link the stately buildings with one another. At the centre of the square is a memorial to Dante from 1865. Archaeological excavations have revealed Roman paving slabs, mosaics and the foundations of several of the ancient city's public buildings.

Coming from the Piazza delle Erbe, you enter the square below the mighty walls of the Palazzo del Comune (also known as the Palazzo della Ragione). The austerity of its Romanesque architecture was softened in 1524 through the addition of Venetian Renaissance reliefs. The façade onto the Piazza dei Signori, only broken by a few windows and arches, is animated by alternating rows of red brick

In the evening the rectangular piazza resembles an atmospherically lit open-air theatre

Dante Alighieri lived in Verona for seven years

and light-coloured tuff stone. An external marble staircase (c. 1450) that was once roofed over, leads up to the former Council Chamber from the inner courtyard surrounded by a row of tall arcades. The Torre dei Lamberti towers above the building (►111).

In 1575 an arch was added over the narrow Via Dante to create an optical link between the Palazzo Comunale and the Palazzo dei Tribunali. The fortress-like, quadrangular building and the defence tower were erected by the much-feared Cansignorio della Scala. The structure was later used as an artillery school and the seat of the Venetian governor. The loggia dates from 1476; the Renaissance portal was created in 1530 by Michele Sanmicheli.

One of the most beautiful Early Renaissance buildings is the two-storey **Loggia del Consiglio** on the north side of the

Verona

piazza that was built in the Venetian style between 1486 and 1493. It has been attributed to the Dominican monk Giovanni Giocondo (also known as Giovanni da Verona, 1433–1515). The rounded arches in the arcade are supported on slender columns. The building is crowned by five statues of famous people from Ancient Verona.

The castellated **Palazzo del Governo** (also known as the Palazzo della Prefettura) closes off the eastern side of the square. It was also a residence of the della Scala family – in this case of Cangrande I. The façade was altered to accommodate an arcade in 1419 and, in 1553, Sanmicheli added the representative portal. Giotto and Altichiero decorated the palace with frescos, of which only sections have survived to this day.

The Scaliger coat of arms includes a flight of steps (ital. *scala*)

TAKING A BREAK

In the square itself try the trattoria/pizzeria **Impero** at no. 8. Alternatively head for the bar and restaurant in **Caffè Dante** (no. 2) housed in a Renaissance building from around 1500 that has now been beautifully restored.

➕ 183 E4

INSIDER INFO

The Scavi Scaligeri, the excavated Roman streets that lie beneath the Palazzo del Capitano, occasionally houses **photographic exhibitions**. This provides the perfect occasion to see both the streets and some works of art.

⑧Piazza delle Erbe

The Piazza delle Erbe, one of Italy's most beautiful squares, lies at the heart of the Old Town and hosts a flower and vegetable market on weekdays.

This was originally the site of the forum in the Roman city. It now lies 4m (13ft) below the present ground level. The Capitello, a podest crowned by a baldachin (16th century), from where important decisions and court rulings were proclaimed, is located on the square. Further to the north is the market fountain with the 'Madonna Verona', a marble Roman statue. Merchants used to gather in the Casa dei Mercanti opposite the Palazzo del Comune that was constructed in 1301 and rebuilt in 1878. North of the Palazzo del Comune are the Case dei Mazzanti behind the passage onto the Piazza dei Signori. The beautiful Renaissance frescos on the façades were commissioned by the Mazzanti family that acquired the buildings in 1517. The Baroque Palazzo Maffei (1668) on the north side of the square houses the tourist information office. Nearby is the Torre del Gardello which boasts the oldest town clock in Verona dating from 1370. A wonderful panoramic view of the square can be had from the 84m (276ft)-high **Torre dei Lamberti** on the other side. A lift whisks visitors to the top from the inner courtyard of the **Palazzo del Comune** (➤ 108).

The Piazza delle Erbe is the city's 'belly'

TAKING A BREAK

The **Mezzaparte** at no. 8a serves the best hot chocolate (and has Wi-Fi), while the **Orchidea** at no. 22 is a good *gelateria* and café.

Insider Tip

✚ 183 E4

Torre dei Lamberti
☎ 045 9 27 30 27 🕔 June–Sep 8:30–8:30, Fri until 11pm; Oct–March 8:30–7:30
🖐 €6

INSIDER INFO

- The Piazza Erbe is oriented northwest/southeast, so the **best time to climb Torre dei Lamberti** for views and for taking photos is late morning when the sun shines along the length of the square.
- On the corner of Piazza Erbe and Via Cappello Juliet fans can buy some 'unique Juliet wine' and countless other Romeo and Juliet souvenirs. The **Cantina di Giulietta** sells 'Cara Giulietta' wine: 07l for €10 upwards.

㉜ San Zeno Maggiore

The large Basilica San Zeno Maggiore, one of the most beautiful Romanesque churches in northern Italy, is flanked by a belltower and a castellated defence tower. The present building was erected in the 12th century over the tomb of the city's patron saint, Zeno, as the church of an influential Benedictine monastery.

Zeno was Bishop of Verona from 362 until 371. He originally came from Africa which explains why the **Gothic seated figure** in the burial church of San Zeno is made of black marble. He was one of the major Early Christian pulpit orators who vehemently defended the teachings of Christ in Veneto in the face of the rapid spread of paganism. Medieval legends praise the care he showed for the poor and the sick as well as his unrelenting work to ward off Arianism and the philosophy in Late Antiquity. When Zeno died on 12 April 371, he left an extensive collection of interpretations of the scriptures in Latin as well as treatises on baptism, the Easter liturgy and Mariology.

The west façade is dominated by a large rose window and a **portal** made by Master Nicolò, a magnum opus of Gothic sculptural art. It is shielded by a projecting baldachin whose columns rest on two stone lions. In the tympanon over the portal, Bishop Zeno hands the banner of the free commune to the people of Verona. The famous **bronze doors** have a wooden core to which the bronze panels were nailed. Stylistic differences show that they were created in two phases. In the scenes depicted on the older panels created around 1100, there is no spatial depth and the figures are not supported on a base; in the later reliefs (c. 1200), a feeling of space is created through the use of perspective. The panels show scenes from the Old and the New Testaments, miracles performed by St Zeno, figures of kings and allegories of virtues. The high central nave has an unusual wooden ceiling (14th century) whereas the raised choir has ribbed vaulting. The **crypt**, laid out like a large lower church, is under the choir. 48 columns with artistically worked capitals support the vaulted ceiling. A balustrade with statues of Christ and the Apostles (*c.* 1260) separates the nave from the choir where the most important work of art in the basilica can be seen – a three-part **altarpiece** with the Virgin Mary in the centre, an early work (1456–1459) by the major Renaissance painter Andrea Mantegna. The painting in the church is however a copy. The glowing

The cloister, built in 1123, can be reached from the northern side nave. The vaulted ceiling was altered in the style of the period in the 14th century. The cloister is dominated by an imposing Romanesque campanile.

UP HIGH ON A CART DRAWN BY OXEN

The city's *carraccio* (a 4-wheeled war altar) once stood in the left nave of the Basilica of San Zeno Maggiore. Drawn by oxen, the waggon preceded the city's troops into battle. On it were relics of the city's patron saint – San Zeno, priests praying for victory and a rebel-rousing band of drums and trumpets to give the soldiers encouragement. The capture of an opponent's *carraccio* was a humiliating blow.

View of the basilica's central aisle. The Romanesque elements in the interior of the church dedicated to the patron saint are monumental but refined at the same time

colours and the impression given of a three-dimensional pictorial space that is continued in the architectural features framing the scene, are characteristic of Mantegna's masterly painting.

TAKING A BREAK

There is a café across from the old tower, on the corner of Vicolo Abbazia, but for something more substantial try the **Trattoria Al Calmiere** further along in the Piazza San Zeno.

 Insider Tip

✚ 182 B4

◎ March–Nov Mon–Sat 8:30–6, Sun 12:30–6; Dec–Feb 10–1, 1:30–5

INSIDER INFO

San Zeno is on the itinerary of every **coach tour** to Verona, but the first coaches do not arrive until mid-morning. As the church opens at 8:30am, arrive early to enjoy a peaceful visit.

At Your Leisure

Only the Scaligers were allowed to cross the Ponte Scaligero

33 Castelvecchio & Ponte Scaligero

The complex on the banks of the Adige, built in the mid 14th century under Cangrande II, comprises two sections – a fortress and barracks facing the city that was to protect the Scaligers more from the Veronese than other enemies, and a palace with the living quarters. Between the two there is a tall defence tower through which you pass to get to the Ponte Scaligero. The wide-arched bridge, completed in 1375 to enable the inhabitants of the Castelvecchio to flee across the Adige in the face of danger, is castellated and has bastions and defence walkways. After the fall of the last Scaliger in 1387, the fortress complex fell into ruin. It was restored in 1923–64 and now houses the **Museo di Castelvecchio**. At this time the former defence tower was given a Venetian-Gothic façade. The historical rooms inside the art museum were designed by the architect, Carlo Scarpa. An impressive collection of artworks by Veronese sculptors and painters from the 12th to the 18th centuries is shown in 29 rooms. Sculptures from the 12th to the 15th centuries are exhibited in the first rooms, followed by examples of Veronese painting (14th/15th centuries), including *Madonna of the Rose Garden* of 1425 and the *Madonna of the Quail* by Pisanello. Other exceptional works from the heyday of Veronese Gothic and Renaissance painting, such as by Turone and Bellini, are also to be seen. Important paintings by Veronese, Tintoretto and Tiepolo, for example, document the 16th and 17th centuries. One of the most important works of art in the museum is on a plinth between the defence tract and the residential wing, namely the ambiguously smiling knight, Cangrande della Scala, on horseback (14th century).
➕ 182 C3

Museo di Castelvecchio
☎ 045 8 06 26 11
🕐 Tue–Sun 8:30–7:30, Mon 1:30–7:30 💶 €6

ROMEO AND JULIET IN VERONA
Love is heaven sent – but sometimes you have to give it a helping hand. As Verona lacks any genuine sites from the tale, these have simply been created instead. Even letters addressed to 'Juliet, Verona, Italy' are answered! Which, of course, is proof that Juliet is alive and well.

34 Tomba di Giulietta

Close to the river in Via del Pontieri, about 350m south of the Arena, is the Tomba di Giulietta, a 14th-century marble sarcophagus, now empty, which tradition has it was the last resting place of Shakespeare's heroine. Legend also says that Romeo and Juliet were married in the Franciscan monastery that once stood here, but there is no more truth in this than in the legend linking Juliet with the sarcophagus in the Baroque chapel. But as with Juliet's House, the site feels right and that feeling is shared by the many who come here to drop love letters in the sarcophagus or coins in the courtyard fountain.

Far removed from the realm of fiction, the medieval frescos in the small **Museo degli Affreschi** adjoining, have their very own stories to tell.

➕ 183 E2

Tomba di Giulietta/Museo degli Affreschi
✉ Via del Pontiere 35 ☎ 045 8 00 03 61
🕐 Mon 1:30–7:30, Tue–Sun 8:30–7:30 💶 €4.50

35 San Fermo Maggiore

North of Juliet's tomb, in a square at the town end of the Ponte Navi, stands the **Church of San Fermo Maggiore**.

Between 1065 and 1138 Benedictine monks built a church

Touching the breasts of the statue of Juliet outside the Casa di Giulietta is said to bring good fortune in matters of the heart

on top of an older building from the 6th century that was dedicated to the two Veronese martyrs Fermo and Rustico (†361). The Franciscans who were granted the church in 1260 changed the three-aisled upper church into a hall church and extended it to the west. To the east, the remarkable choir group was created that is characterised by the contrasting Gothic main choir with its towering lancet windows and the four small Romanesque apses. A tour of the Gothic upper church (13th/14th centuries) is recommended before entering the Romanesque lower church (11th/12th centuries). The sculptures, wooden ceiling and the frescos in the upper church are outstanding. By contrast, the lower church is a simple, dignified, vaulted structure. Here too there are some good frescos.

➕ 183 F3

36 Casa di Giulietta

Year in, year out, some three million people make their way to Verona to

View from Castel San Pietro of the Adige and Verona's city centre

see for themselves the city in which William Shakespeare placed what is probably the most famous love story in literature. It is possible that the writer had heard the Italian saying – attributed to Giordano Bruno: "Se non è vero, è (molto) ben trovato" (If it is not true, it is (certainly) well conceived). At any rate, Verona makes a good living from Shakespeare's play and, to give the fictive story a real location, Antonio Avena – the director of Verona's museums at the beginning of the 20th century – had a balcony made from a sarcophagus in the museum depot and added it to the house of the Cappello family. The name of this dynasty of merchants from the 13th century is remotely reminiscent of Juliet's family, the Capuletis. The Gothic window and the portal with its pointed arch were also taken from other buildings and so the stage set was completed. Two roads further north, in the Via Arche Scaligere, is the 'Casa di Romeo' – a remnant of a former town palace belonging to the Montecchi (Montague) family. This is really where they did live and, if one of their offspring was ever called Romeo, who knows if he loved a girl called Juliet?

✚ 183 E4 ✉ Via Capello 23
☎ 045 8 03 43 03
🕐 Mon 1:30–7:30, Tue–Sun 9–7 💶 €5

🔢37 Santa Maria Antica

The passage between the Palazzo del Governo and the Palazzo dei Tribunali leads from the Piazza dei Signori to the small, three-aisled church of Santa Maria Antica (12th century), the Scaliger's private church. Above the portal is the sarcophagus of Cangrande I (†1329), borne by two dogs that are a play on the ruler's name – Cangrande, meaning 'large dog'. A copy of an unusual statue of a laughing equestrian figure (the original is in Castelvecchio) can be seen over the baldachin above the tomb. The Gothic tombs of other members of the della Scala are in the family cemetery next to the church (Arche Scaligere). The artistically worked railings around the cemetery are from the 14th century. The cemetery itself boasts the sarcophagus of Mastinos II († 1351) and the magnificent, exquisitely fashioned tomb of Cansignorio († 1375). Both have richly decorated baldachins with pyramidal roofs, crowned by equestrian figures of the respective Scaligers.

✚ 183 F4

🔢38 Sant'Anastasia

The church of Sant'Anastasia, close to the bank of the River Adige, is also reached from the Piazza dei

Signori down a narrow alleyway. This mighty brick building – the largest Gothic church in Verona – was the Dominican monastery church. It was started in 1290 but not completed until 1481. From the other side of the Adige, you can get a good view not only of the delicately balanced architecture of the belltower but also of the choir section with its six polygonal chapels. The overall impression one has of the dark interior, divided into three aisles by tall columns, is dictated by the coloured floor, the red marble pillars and the ornamental painting of the cupola. The two stoups (holy water fonts) on the first pair of columns are supported by hunched figures called the 'due gobbi'. The figure on the left is from 1500 and is attributed to Caliari, the father of the famous Paolo Veronese. The figure on the right is nine years older. The tomb of the *condottiere* Cortesia Serego of 1429, a field marshal under the Scaligers, is in the main choir. The chapels to the left and right of the main choir have excellent Late Gothic frescos. The southernmost chapel is especially interesting as a superb votive fresco by Altichiero dating from around 1390 embellishes the wall surrounding the tomb of Federico Cavalli. The fresco *St George and the Princess*, that

Pisanello painted around 1435 above the arch to the first chapel on the right of the main entrance, is considered a masterpiece of Upper Italian painting, in which the Late Gothic style is not only perfected but, at the same time, superseded. This can readily be seen in the depiction of the horse where the extreme, foreshortened perspective already hints at the spatial feeling found in Renaissance painting.

➕ 183 F4

39 Duomo

Externally, Verona's cathedral is a Romanesque basilica. The ornamental work is concentrated primarily around the main portal that is considered to be the work of Maestro Nicolò. In addition to prophets, two figures of warriors can be seen on the columns to the side of the portal. These are reputedly Roland and Olivier, two *paladine* (peers) in Charlemagne's court. The monumental interior, subdivided by groups of columns into three aisles of almost equal height, is characterised by later modifications, especially those of the 15th and early 16th centuries. Among the most impressive works of art inside the cathedral is the large-format retable in the first chapel on the north aisle which includes one version of Titian's painting *The Assumption* (c. 1540).

The magnificent tombs of the Scaliger dynasty tell of the ebb and flow of time and power

Verona

+ 183 E5 **☎** 045 59 28 13
◷ March–Oct Mon–Sat 10–5:30; Nov–Feb
Tue–Sat 10–4, Sun and public holidays 1:30–5

40 Museo Archeologico & Teatro Romano

On the other side of the Ponte della Pietra – one of two Roman bridges in the city – the rows of seats in the former Roman theatre. dating from the time of Emperor Augustus (63BC–14AD) climb the slope below the Castel San Pietro. Between July and September the theatre is used for concerts, ballet performances and plays. The church of Santi Siro e Libera (10th century) with its Baroque marble steps and late medieval San Girolamo monastery are located above the seating area. The monastery now houses the archaeological museum (**Museo Archeologico**).

+ 183 F5 **✉** Via Redentore 2
☎ 045 8 00 03 60
◷ Tue–Sun 9–7:30 **◉** €6

41 Giardino Giusti

The Porta Organa leads to the Palazzo Giusti (1580). The adjoining Renaissance garden is a little paradise. Beyond a hedge maze with statues peaking over the tops and the sound of bubbling water features, the park stretches up the slope, interspersed with narrow paths that pass through grottoes and old pavilions. On the hillside there is a more natural area following a re-design in the 19th century. The cypresses are such a feature of this section that Goethe is said to have picked some twigs from them during his visit as a souvenir.

+ 183 off F5 **✉** Via Giardino Giusti 2
☎ 045 8 03 40 29 **◷** April–Sep daily 9–8;
Oct–March daily 9–7 **✋** €7

42 San Giorgio in Braida

If, instead of turning right at the end of the Ponte Pietra, you bear left beside the river you will reach the domed church of San Giorgio in Braida. Built in the 15th century on the site of an earlier church, the prominent dome was added by Sanmicheli 200 years later. Inside there are a number of fine artworks, including what many believe to be Paolo Veronese's masterpiece, *The Martyrdom of St George*, and a *Baptism of Christ* by Jacopo Tintoretto.

+ 185 E5

Box hedging and cypress trees in the typically Italianate Giusti Gardens

Where to...
Stay

Prices
Expect to pay per double room, per night
€ under €80   €€ €80–€130   €€€ over €130

Hotel Accademia €€€
Right at the heart of the historic centre, the Accademia is just a short walk from Juliet's House. It occupies a 17th-century *palazzo* and combines antique furnishings with modern facilities. The rooms are elegant and well appointed and the restaurant is excellent.
✚ 183 E3 ✉ Via Scala 12
☎ 045 59 62 22; www.hotelaccademiaverona.it

Bologna €€
In a lovely, fully renovated, old building in a quiet area just a short walk from the Arena. Well-appointed rooms, friendly staff and secure parking.
✚ 183 D3 ✉ Piazzetta Sealette Rubiani 3
☎ 045 8 00 68 30; www.hotelbologna.vr.it

De Capuleti €€
Close to Juliet's tomb and so about 10 minutes' walk from the Arena, this hotel is family run and very friendly. It has been modernised to a high standard. Secure parking.
✚ 183 E2 ✉ Via del Pontiere 26
☎ 045 8 00 01 54; www.hotelcapuleti.it

Due Torri Hotel €€€
A 13th-century *palazzo* close to the church of Sant'Anastasia is now Verona's most exclusive hotel. The public rooms with their arches and stylish bedrooms are the height of elegance and every possible convenience is provided. The restaurant is, as would be expected, first class.
✚ 183 F4 ✉ Piazza Sant'Anastasia 4
☎ 045 59 50 44;
hotelduetorri.duetorrihotels.com

Giulietta e Romeo €€
Pretty hotel right behind the Arena. For here, everything can be reached on foot. Or, if you prefer, you can borrow a bicycle free of charge. *Insider Tip*
✚ 183 E3 ✉ Vicolo Tre Marchetti 3
☎ 045 8 00 35 54; www.giuliettaeromeo.com

Grand Hotel €€€
The Grand is very well positioned on the road linking the city centre with the A4 *autostrada* and is just a few minutes' walk from the Piazza Bra. There is a delightful private courtyard garden.
✚ 183 D2 ✉ Corso Porta Nuova 105
☎ 045 59 56 00; www.grandhotel.vr.it

San Marco €€€
Close to San Zeno Maggiore and so a 20-minute walk, or short bus ride, from the main centre. Breakfast is served in the garden. There is also a pool.
✚ 182 off A3 ✉ Via Longhena 42
☎ 045 56 90 11; www.sanmarco.vr.it

Verona €€
Well-appointed rooms and tastefully furnished public areas.
✚ 199 D2 ✉ Corso Porta Nuova 47/49
☎ 045 59 59 44; www.hotelverona.it

Hotel Veronesi La Torre €€€
This prettily renovated former monastery is a few miles from the centre. Tip: for those visiting during the festival season there are often rooms still to be had here.
✚ 181 D1 ✉ Via Monte Baldo 22, VE-Dossobuono di Villafranca
☎ 045 8 60 48 11; www.hotelveronesilatorre.it

Where to...
Eat and Drink

Prices
Expect to pay for a three-course meal for one, excluding drinks and service
€ under €30   € €30–€60   €€€ over €60

Al Capitan della Cittadella €€€
This fish restaurant is not cheap but the food is in a class of its own.
🚼 183 D2 ✉ Piazza Cittadella 7
☎ 045 59 51 57; www.alcapitan.it
🕒 Closed Sun, Mon

Al Cristo €€
Close to the Ponte Nuovo and so a little distance from the city centre, this restored 16th-century *palazzo* is worth the walk for its delightful atmosphere. Good fish and meat dishes served on a terrific terrace.
🚼 183 F4 ✉ Piazzetta Peschiera 6
☎ 045 59 42 87; www.ristorantealcristo.it
🕒 Closed Mon

Antica Bottega del Vino €€
Tucked away off the Via Mazzini, the Antica Bottega del Vino is wonderfully atmospheric with its bottle-lined walls. Specialities include the chef's tortellini, polenta dishes and horse meat. The wine list runs to about 100 pages. The service is superb.
🚼 183 E3 ✉ Via Scudo di Francia 3
☎ 045 8 0045 35; www.bottegavini.it
🕒 Closed Tue except during the opera season

Arche €€€
One of the best restaurants in Verona, with a prime position close to the Scaligeri tombs. Fresh fish arrives daily for the evening menu which comprises traditional dishes with a modern twist. The steamed turbot fillet on a bed of spinach in a ginger sauce is delicious.
🚼 183 E4 ✉ Via Arche Scaligere 6
☎ 045 8 00 74 15; www.ristorantearche.com
🕒 Closed Sun and Mon lunch

La Costa in Bra €
La Costa claims to be the oldest pizzeria in town. The non-pizza menu is limited, but excellent. Good service and in summer you can eat alfresco.
🚼 183 D3 ✉ Piazza Bra 2
☎ 045 59 74 68; www.lacostainbra.it

Il Desco €€€
The best 2-star cuisine in a wonderfully atmospheric setting. A fantastic place with prices to match. The tasting menu costs €135. Booking essential.
🚼 183 F3 ✉ Via Dietro San Sebastiano 7
☎ 045 59 53 58
🕒 Closed Sun and Mon

Il Dolmen €€
Stone archways here do indeed recall a neolithic burial chamber despite the garden setting. Fish dishes a speciality. Long wine list.
🚼 183 E2
✉ Vicolo Cieco San Pietro Incarnario 5/7
☎ 045 80 07 45 🕒 Closed Mon

Greppia €€
Close to Via Cappello and Piazza Erbe in a quiet square. Veronese dishes.
🚼 183 E4 ✉ Vicolo Samaritana 3c
☎ 045 8 00 45 77 🕒 Closed Mon.
Also closed for two weeks in Jan and June

Mondodoro € *Insider Tip*
Fine old *osteria* just off Via Mazzini offering year-round al fresco dining. Veronese menu and local wines.
🚼 183 E4 ✉ Via Mondo d'Oro 4
☎ 045 8 03 26 79; www.osteriamondodoro.it
🕒 Closed Mon

Where to...
Shop

VIA MAZZINI

For general shopping, the best place is Via Mazzini and the nearby streets. Via Mazzini itself is home to Gucci, Versace, Max Mara, Marinarinaldi, Bulgari and Cartier, among others. But there are many less internationally famous brands that are worth visiting too. For young fashions try **Promod**, **Pimkie** and **Oltre**. For shoes and bags look at **Rossetti**, **Bruschi** and **Furla**. **Erbovoglio** is excellent for children's clothes and shoes. **Al Duca d'Aosta** has high-quality clothes and shoes for both men and women. A huge range of leather goods can be found at **Campana**, with everything from wallets to luggage. **Fiorucci** and **Upim**, Verona's biggest department stores, are also in Via Mazzini (no. 6 and no. 10).

LEATHER

As well as the Via Mazzini shops try **Principe** (on the corner of Via Alberto Mario and Piazzetta Scalette Rubiani). There is also **Bettanin & Venturi** (Vicolo Morette 4) where shoes have been made for almost 150 years, and **Folli Follie** (Via Oberdan 9a/b) for shoes and bags.

FASHION

Corso Porta Borsari has many elegant fashion shops such as **Carlo Bottico** and **Just Cavalli** for women, while **Dismero** at no. 53, **Patrizia Pepe** and **iam** design for a younger, trendier clientele. Also of note are **Mariella Burani** at no. 28 and **Stizzoli**, next door at no. 30, both offering classically elegant ladies' fashions as well as something a little different. For something more avant garde, go to **Lazzari** (Piazza Erbe 15). **Class Country** (Via San Rochetto 6) has traditional menswear, as does **Class Uomo** at no. 13b in the same street. **Camicissima** (Piazza Bra 3) has a large range of inexpensive men's shirts.

GALLERIA RIVOLI

The passage near the Piazza Bra has several shops including **Antiqua** for antiques, **Giancarlo** for shoes and bags, **La Dispensa Mamma Pia** for wine and olive oil and **Nereo Stevanella** for elegant silver jewellery.

ANTIQUES

The best area for antiques is **Corso Sant'Anastasia** and the adjacent streets. There are also good shops closer to the *duomo*. However, be cautious, as there is a thriving trade in reproductions.

JEWELLERY

Damiani has an outlet at no. 59 Via Mazzini and it is also worth visiting **G&G Amighini** (Piazzetta Monte 3), which specialises in silver.

OUT OF TOWN

North of Verona, in the Centro Commerciale in Affi, is a warehouse outlet selling a wide range of Italian clothing and footwear.

MARKETS

There is a daily market on the **Piazza Erbe**. There are also markets on the **Piazza San Zeno** on Tuesdays and Fridays, on the **Piazza Isolo** on Tuesdays and on the **Piazza Santa Toscana** on Wednesdays and Fridays. Every third Saturday of the month there are antiques, objets d'art and crafts on the **Piazza San Zeno**.

Where to…
Go Out

CARNIVAL

Verona carnival is one of the oldest in Italy, dating back to the early 16th century. It is held in the early spring. Contact the tourist information office for exact dates. The highlight of the event is the last Friday before Shrove Tuesday, known as the **Bacanal del Gnoco**, at which the Papa del Gnoco, holding a huge potato dumpling on a fork, takes charge.

FESTIVALS

There is an **international film festival** in the city in April. From June to August there are Shakespearean plays (performed in Italian) in the Roman amphitheatre.

At Christmas the **Festa di Santa Lucia** is held, with seasonal street markets on the Piazza Bra and Via Roma. The Piazza Bra celebrations include displays of cribs from around the world in the arcades of the Arena.

The **Opera Festival** held in the Arena from mid June until the beginning of September is world famous. Book ahead (tel: 045 8 00 51 51) to be sure of a ticket. 'Real' fans tend to go for the – cheaper – tiered seats. Hotels can be busy too, so it is worth booking in advance.

THEATRE

As well as the Roman amphitheatre there are several other theatres in the city. The **Teatro Nuovo** has a famous drama festival from December to April, whereas operas are staged at the **Teatro Filarmonico** from February to April.

NIGHTLIFE

The Veronese have their own version of a British 'pub-crawl' – andar per goti, 'going for a Gothic'. There are, consequently, a large number of bars, many of them with live music, particularly at weekends. For the best, head for the Piazza Bra or Piazza Erbe.

The city is surprisingly short of discos and nightclubs. Popular at the moment are **Dorian Gray**, a stylish disco at Via Belobono 13, the **Atlantis Pub** (Piazza Cittadella 7) with regular live music and **Alter Ego** (Via Torricelle).

There are, however, several out-of-town nightspots. **Berfei's Club** is a disco/restaurant (Via Lussemburgo 1) off the road towards the A4 autostrada (Verona South exit). Alternatively, try **Night City Club** (Via Bresciana 1f) which is located off the SS11 Verona–Peschiera road.

HITS FOR KIDS

The **Arena** offers the possibility of treading ground once trodden by gladiators and Castelvecchio and its weaponry also appeals to most children. Areas around the city's old defensive walls have been made into parks and two of these have good children's playgrounds – **Arsenale** near Castelvecchio and **Raggio di Sole** near Porta Nuovo.

The **La Spiaggia** (ex **Tropic del SoloSole) @ Village**, close to Bussolengo, northwest of Verona, has a vast swimming pool with rock towers and other 'natural' features, and a roller-skating rink. Although it is not specifically aimed at children, most will enjoy it.

The **Parco Natura Viva**, a combination of a safari park and a zoo, is also in Bussolengo and incorporates a dinosaur park with life-sized models.

Northern Lombardy

 **Little Treats**

Cold and Delicious

The famous **stracciatella ice cream** was first made in Bergamo (► 128). The original can be sampled at the Gelateria Marianna, Via Colle Aperto 4.

Southern Fruit from the North

On traffic-free **Monte Isola** (► 134) on Lake Iseo you'll be in for a big surprise. Oranges, lemons, kiwis and bananas all grow on the sheltered south side of the island.

Golden Risotto

The **Ristorante Gualtiero Marchesi** in Erbusco on Lake Iseo (► 133) – with two Michelin stars, one of the best restaurants in Italy – is famous for its risotto decorated with gold leaf.

Getting Your Bearings

To this day Bergamo and Brescia have remained important centres at the point where old trade routes cross and the southern Alps run into the plain of the River Po. Their enchanting Old Towns have many historical relics dating from Antiquity up to the heyday of the Venetian Republic. The area around Lago d'Iseo is picturesque. Val Camonica is a UNESCO World Heritage Site famous for its rock drawings.

Brescia is Lombardy's second largest city after Milan, a prosperous place with interesting Roman remains, some good Renaissance buildings and a museum housing some of the finest art-historical treasures in Italy. Visitors, howerver, first have to pass through less attractive industrial areas and cope with the permanent traffic jams that plague the outskirts of the city until they can get closer to the real sights.

Bergamo is a city with two totally different faces. On the plain is the sprawling Città Bassa, the busy lower town of modern buildings and industry. On a ridge, some 120m above the River Serio, is the Città Alta, the medieval upper town with a labyrinth of narrow alleyways and lots of art treasures.

North of Bergamo and Brescia beautiful valleys cut into the Alpine foothills; to the east is Val Camonica, with a renowned thermal spa and fascinating prehistoric drawings in the Parco Nazionale delle Incisioni Rupestri.

TOP 10

⭐9 Bergamo ► 128
⭐10 Lago d'Iseo ► 133

Don't Miss

43 Brescia ► 136

At Your Leisure

44 Boario Terme ► 139
45 Breno ► 139
46 Capo di Ponte ► 140

Left: The 'Mille Miglia' road endurance race was a classic event unparalleled at the time. The route, some '1000 Miles' long, ran from Brescia to Rome and back along largely unmade country roads. Since 1977, the new 'Mille Miglia Storica' has revived this veteran car race much to the joy of enthusiasts of sports and vintage cars. If you miss the race held annually in May that starts in Brescia, you can always visit the Museo Mille Miglia (www.museomillemiglia.it) which is also in Brescia and marvel at the most beautiful old timers that participate in the race.

Northern Lombardy

Three Perfect Days

This suggested route takes you to some of the most interesting sights in northern Lombardy over a three-day period and ensures that you will not miss any of the highlights. For more information see the main entries (► 128–140).

Day One

Morning

Start your day in ⭐**Bergamo**'s Città Bassa (Lower City), saying hello to Donizetti outside the theatre named in his honour and having a look at the shops in the **Sentierone** (► 129). Then follow the Via Roma/Via Vittorio Emanuele II to reach the cable-car to the Città Alta (Upper City), the Old Town. Head straight up to the Piazza Vecchia, then visit the *duomo*, Santa Maria Maggiore and the **Cappella Colleoni** (► 130). Have lunch in one of the restaurants on the Piazza Vecchia – perhaps the **Caffè del Tasso**.

Afternoon

From the Piazza Vecchia follow the Via Gombito back towards the cable-car upper station, but instead of riding down follow the road downhill past the Rocca, to your left, to reach an open area where you can see the Old Town walls and look north to the alpine foothills. Turn right through the Porta Sant'Agostino and then bear left along the Via di Noca to reach the **Accademia Carrara** (► 129). You can enjoy the rest of the afternoon admiring the collection of works by Bellini, Botticelli, Canaletto, Raphael, Tiepolo and many others. Or, if contemporary art is more your line, pay a visit to the **Galleria d'Arte Moderna e Contemporanea** right next to the Neo-Classical seat of the Accademia.

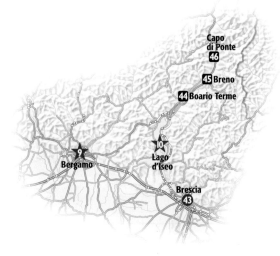

Evening

In the evening walk back up to the Piazza Vecchia and have dinner in the restaurant **Colleoni e dell'Angelo**, for example, which serves excellent food in a beautiful setting. By the time you have finished eating the square will be floodlit.

Day Two

Morning

Travel to **43 Brescia**, arriving in the late morning. Start your exploration of the town on the **Piazza della Vittoria** (➤ 138) with its Rationalism architecture, then continue north to Piazza della Loggia to enjoy the medieval buildings. You will probably want to have lunch here – and there are few better places in town.

Afternoon

Now take the passage-way beneath the clock tower to reach Piazza Paolo VI and Brescia's **twin cathedrals** (right, ➤ 137). It is worth visiting each for their art treasures. After your visit walk past the Broletto and turn right along Via dei Musei to see the best of the Roman remains – the Capitoline Temple – and to visit the town museum.

Evening

If you are staying the night in Brescia rather than on Lake Iseo, take an early-evening stroll up onto the Colle Cidneo to enjoy the parkland and the views of the old fortress. Then head back down to the Old Town to enjoy a meal, perhaps at **La Sosta** in Via San Martino della Battaglia.

Day Three

Morning

Make an early start and follow the eastern shore of ⭐**Lago d'Iseo** (➤ 133), taking the road along the Val Camonica from Pisogne to reach **44 Boario Terme** (➤ 139) in time for lunch, for example at **Airone** at Via Nazionale 15.

Afternoon

After a quick exploration of the town, continue along the main valley road to reach **46 Capo di Ponte** (➤ 140) where you will want to explore some of the rock engravings on foot as well as visit the museum.

Evening

You can either return to Brescia or, if staying nearby, you might drive back to Lake Iseo and watch the sun go down behind the hills along the western shore.

⭐ Bergamo

The Città Alta, protected by its walls and bastions, perches like an eyrie above Bergamo's modern Città Bassa. Bustling activity down below; churches, *palazzi* and *piazze* from days of old up high. Bergamo is perfect for those seeking art and architectural highlights as well as for those who love the everyday life of an Italian metropolis. These two contrasting worlds are conveniently linked by a funicular.

Città Bassa

At the centre of Bergamo's lower town is the **Piazza Matteotti**, its gardens split by Viale Roma which – changing names in both directions – links the upper town with the railway station. On one side of Viale Roma, Piazza Matteotti leads to Via XX Septembre, the city's main shopping street. On the other side stands the **Teatro Donizetti**. Built in the 18th century to accommodate 1300 people, the theatre was given a new façade and a new name to celebrate the 100th anniversary of the birth of Bergamo's most famous son, the composer Gaetano Donizetti (1797–1848). Beyond the theatre is the Piazza Cavour where Donizetti

The interior of the cathedral in Bergamo is a joy for lovers of Baroque architecture

View over the *funicolare* of the lower town, the Città Bassa

is depicted listening thoughtfully to Melpomene – the muse of song – as she plays her lyre.

Opposite the theatre is the **Sentierone**, the 'Big Path' which, with its cafés and shops, is a favourite among the people of the city. The Sentierone forms part of Via Torquato Tasso. If you like religious art, follow this away from the city centre to see works by the Venetian Lorenzo Lotto (c. 1480–1556). The altarpiece of the Madonna in the church of **San Bartolomeo** (to the left) is one of his master-pieces and there are other works in the churches of Santo Spirito and San Bernardino further along the road.

On the Piazza G. Carrara, the **Accademia Carrara** – housed in a Late Classical building from 1796 – exhibits exceptional works by artists from Italian and international schools from the 15th to the 18th centuries. Among the highlights are portraits by Giuliano de'Medici (Botticelli) and Lionello d'Este (Pisanello) as well as the *Holy Family and St Catherine of Siena* by Lorenzo Lotto. The ad-joining **Galleria d'Arte Moderna e Contemporanea** (Via San Tomaso 53) is devoted to contemporary art.

Città Alta

To access the pedestrianised upper town, follow Viale Roma which becomes Via Vittorio Emanuele II to the lower station of the funicular railway. In one sense this is a short ride, but in another it is the opposite. You climb on board and a few minutes later you have gone back 500 years in time, to a city of Renaissance Italy where all but essential vehicles are excluded.

From the funicular's top station cross the small square and take the narrow, winding Via Gombito uphill, passing the square and the austere 12th-century Torre Gombito to reach the **Piazza Vecchia**, one of the most enchanting squares in northern Italy. To your right as you enter is the **Palazzo Nuovo**, designed by the celebrated Renaissance architect Vincenzo Scamozzi (1552–1616) and modelled on the Sansovino library in Venice. It also houses an im-portant library.

To the left, at the centre of the square, is the **Contarini Fountain**, presented to the town by Alvese Contarini, its

Northern Lombardy

Venetian *podestá* (governor), in 1780. Its lions, symbols of the Venetian Republic, politely hold chains in their mouths. Only 16 years later the inhabitants of Bergamo decided the chains of Venice were too much to bear and they tore the Venetian lion from the façade of the Torre Civica.

The **Palazzo della Ragione** (also known as the Palazzo Vecchio) dominates the opposite side of the square from the Palazzo Nuovo. It was rebuilt in the 16th century after a fire. The statue beside its central portico is of the poet Torquato Tasso (1544–95), about whom Goethe wrote a play and whose father came from Bergamo. Beside the *palazzo* is the **Torre Civica**, the old city's *campanile*, begun in the 11th century but not completed for 400 years.

Go through the arcades of the Palazzo della Ragione to reach the Piazza del Duomo, the oldest part of Bergamo. To the left is the cathedral of **San Vincenzo** with a neo-Classical façade and an impressive dome. The *duomo* is so hemmed in by other buildings that it is difficult to view it in its entirety. Inside, there are several fine works of art, including *The Martyrdom of St John* by Tiepolo and bronze angels by Antonio Fontana.

Despite being the city's cathedral, the *duomo* is outshone by the **Church of Santa Maria Maggiore,** beside it. Built in the 12th century by a city exhausted by war, plague and drought, and in need of spiritual assistance, it is plain on the outside but vast and sumptuous inside. The **Cappella Colleoni** with its richly decorated Renaissance façade of black, white and red marble adjoins the north porch. In 1472 Bartolomeo Colleoni, a mercenary who fought for Milan, Naples and Venice, commissioned Giovanni Antonio Amadeo to build a family mausoleum and chapel. Amadeo also created the tombs of the Colleoni family inside. The cupola frescos by Tiepolo (1789) are also noteworthy as

From the Torre Civica, also known as the Campanone, that towers 54m (177ft) above the Piazza Vecchia, there are wonderful views over the rooftops

Bergamo

is the *Holy Family* by the Swiss painter Angelika Kaufmann (1789).

Next to Santa Maria Maggiore is the 14th-century polygonal baptistry which originally stood inside the church but was taken down and reconstructed in its present position some 200 years ago.

Thee old streets off the Piazza del Duomo are best explored at random. Music lovers may want to see the **birthplace of Gaetano Donizetti** at 14 Via Borgo Canale or the museum dedicated to the composer at 9 Via Arena that includes personal objects and furnishings from Donizetti's home. Nature lovers can head for the **Museo de Scienze Naturali e Caffi** (Natural History Museum), housed in the 14th-century Visconti Cittadella along with the **Museo Civico Archeologico** (Archaeology Museum).

TAKING A BREAK

Depending on where you are: in the upper town head for **Caffè del Tasso** on the Piazza Vecchia, if you are in the lower town then the **Balzer** at Portici Sentierone 41 has excellent snacks, cakes and coffee.

 Insider Tip

The Piazza Vecchia to the south of the Palazzo della Ragione, the former town hall, is the picturesque heart of the Old Town

✚ 178 A3

Torre Civica
☎ 035 24 22 26 🕙 April–Oct Tue–Sun 9:30–7, Sat, hol. 9:30–9:30; Nov–March Sat, hol. 9:30–4:30 💶 €3

Capella Colleoni
☎ 035 21 00 61 🕙 March–Oct Tue–Sun 9–12:30, 2–6:30; Nov–Feb Tue–Sun 9–12:30, 2–4:30 💶 Free

Northern Lombardy

Donizetti's Birthplace
☎ 035 23 73 74 ⏱ Jun–Sep Tue–Sun 9:30–1, 2–5:30;
Oct–May Tue–Fri 9:30–1, Sat, hol. 9:30–1, 2–5:30 💰 €2

Museo Donizettiano
✉ Via Arena 9 ☎ 035 39 92 69 ⏱ Jun–Sep Tue–Sun 9:30–1, 2–5:30;
Oct–May 9:30–1, Sat–Sun 9:30–1, 2–4:30 💰 €4

Museo di Scienze Naturali e 'Enrico Caffi'
✉ Piazza Cittadella 10 ☎ 035 28 60 11
⏱ April–Sep Tue–Fri 9–12:30, 2:30–6, Sat–Sun 9–7;
Oct–March Tue–Sun 9–12:30, 2:30–5:30 💰 Free

Museo Civico Archeologico
✉ Piazza Cittadella 10 ☎ 035 24 28 39
⏱ April–Sep Tue–Fri 9–12:30, 2:30–6, Sat–Sun 9–7;
Oct–March Tue–Sun 9–12:30, 2:30–6 💰 Free

Accademia Carrara
✉ Piazza Carrara 82a ☎ 035 39 96 77 ⏱ Tue–Sun 10–1, 3–6:45 💰 €5

Galleria d'Arte Moderna e Contemporanea
✉ Via San Tomaso 53 ☎ 035 39 95 28
⏱ April–Sep Tue–Sun 10–1, 3–6:45; Oct–March Tue–Sun 9:30–1, 2:30–5:45
💰 Free (except when there is an exhibition)

The Crespi d'Adda settlement is divided by a straight road. On the one side is the mill and, on the other side, roads lead off to the residential area with uniformly designed houses for the workers

INSIDER INFO

Crespi d'Adda – an historical model company town in Capriate San Gervasio in the province of Bergamo – is an early example of the social commitment of enlightened industrialists. It was built from 1878 by the textile manufacturer Cristoforo Crespi and his son, Silvio, on a landscaped site not far from the River Adda which provided the mills and settlement with sufficient water. In the 1920s, more than 3000 workers were still employed here. The workers' estate – now a UNESCO World Heritage Site – includes a school, an infirmary, a wash house and a church. It is still inhabited and has largely retained its original character.

⭐🔟 Lago d'Iseo

The 20.4km (12.7mi) long and only up to 4.1km (2.5mi) wide Lake Iseo is surrounded by the high mountain ranges of the Bergamasque Alps. Its characteristically steep banks mean that swimming is only possible at a few spots but the landscape is extremely attractive. Picturesquely located in the middle of the lake is Monte Isola that rises to a height of some 450m (1476ft), with idyllic villages as well as olive groves, cherry and chestnut trees.

View from Sulzano on the eastern shore over Lake Ideo, bathed in the gentle light of the evening sun

You should plan a good two days for a trip around Lago d'Iseo – or Sebino as it is also called – to take in its very varied scenery, to be able to enjoy leisurely strolls around the little villages and a quick visit to idyllic, car-free Monte Isola. Breathtaking views can be had from the steep west side of the lake and its craggy cliffs. On the eastern shore there are small fishing harbours, Romanesque churches and promenades lined with oleaders and palm trees.

The main town, **Iseo**, on the southern shore, has a beautiful medieval centre with inviting squares and twisty lanes that wind their way up the slope, as well as some good shops. Castello Oldofredi (11th century), now home to a cultural centre, lies above the Old Town. From here you get a view of the roofs of the houses and *palazzi* as well as of the several noteworthy churches from the 11th to the 17th centuries. Ferries depart from the harbour to all the larger settlements on the lake.

To the southwest of Iseo, stretching as far as Clusane, is the **Torbiere del Sebino** nature reserve – a peat bog with rare plants, birds and fish. Slightly above Torbiere is the convent San Pietro in Lamosa, founded in the 11th century by Cluniac monks, with frescos from the 16th century.

Northern Lombardy

Clusane, right on the shore of the lake, is a quiet fishing village with a surprisingly large castle (14th century) with a lovely Renaissance loggia. Clusane is well known for its good fish restaurants.

Near Iseo is **Sarnico**, to the west of Clusane, the largest tourist resort on the lake with good watersports facilities. Good fish restaurants can be found here as well. The Art Deco villas in the Old Town and the surrounding area – among the most beautiful in the whole of Lombardy – are especially attractive.

In the extreme northwest of the lake, lively **Lovere** climbs up the slope from the lakeside. There is a long promenade offering lovely views over the water to the snow-capped mountains in the far distance and a medieval town centre with pretty alleyways and old towers. The **Galleria dell' Accademia Tadini** boasts paintings from the 14th century to the present day, sculptures, Flemish wall-hangings, porcelain and archaeological finds. A few miles east of Lovere it is well worth stopping in **Pisogne** to look at the church of Santa Maria della Neve (15th century) which has an impressive cycle of frescos by Girolamo Romanino from the 16th century. The three town gates date from the Middle Ages.

Monte Isola

An excursion to the traffic-free fishermen's island of Monte Isola is an unforgettable experience. It rises some 450m (1476ft) above the water and covers a good 9km² (3.5mi²). As such, Monte Isola is the largest lake island in southern Europe and has a population of about 1700 who live in the little villages. The main centre on the island is the particularly idyllic village Peschiera Maraglio set against a green backdrop of olive, cherry and chestnut trees. Twisting paths lead from each of the eleven villages to the next. There is also a bus link. The pilgrimage church of **Madonna della Ceriola** perches on the top of the island.

Monte Isola that rises more or less out of the middle of the lake is the real attraction of Lago d'Iseo

Grapes awaiting harvesting in the wine-growing district of Franciacorta, famous in particular for its good sparkling white wines

TAKING A BREAK

In Iseo the best options are on the Piazza Garibaldi. For a meal try **Osteria Antico Melone**, with its short menu of local specialities. At the northern end of the lake the best choice is a café in Pisogne's arcaded **Piazza del Mercato**.

🗺 179 D3

Galleria dell'Accademia Tadini
✉ Palazzo dell'Accademia, Via Tadini, 40 (Lungolago), Lovere
☎ 035 96 27 80; www.accademiatadini.it
🕐 May–Sep Tue–Sat 3–7, Sun 10–noon, 3–7;
Oct–April Sat 3–7, Sun 10–noon, 3–7 💶 €7

INSIDER INFO

- An **historical railway** runs between Bergamo and Lago d'Iseo. The type 940-022 engine pulls the old wooden carriages at a gentle pace through the beautiful country-side of Lombardy. Special wine-tasting trips focussing on regional produce can also be booked. Information: tel. 030 7 40 28 51; www.ferrovieturistiche.it.
- On the road to Zone from Marone, on the eastern shore, just below the village of Cislano, look north to see the extraordinary **Piramidi di Erosione**. These spires of earthy conglomerate, some topped by huge boulders, were formed by glacial erosion.
- A special grape grows in the hilly landscape to the south of Lake Iseo. **Franciacorta** is Italy's most important area for the production of *spumante* made using the traditional bottle fermentation method. An 80km (49mi)-long wine route (www.stradadelfrancia corta.it) takes you not only to the wine growers but also to picturesquely situated monasteries such as the Romanesque Cluniac convent of San Pietro in Lamosa.

㊸ Brescia

With a population of around 195,000, Brescia is Lombardy's second largest city after Milan. The city was heavily bombed in World War II and so it is all the more surprising to discover a historic centre with lots of cultural sites spanning almost 2000 years of history. The former convent of Santa Giulia dates from the Lombard period. Today, it is home to some especially noteworthy museums and, together with the excavation sites nearby, is a UNESCO World Heritage Site.

Brescia was the important centre, Colonia Civica Augusta, in Roman days. The Roman **Capitolium**, however, was largely buried under buildings erected in the following centuries. The Capitoline Temple (1st century), with several mosaics and a Corinthian portico, and the adjoining theatre have been excavated and partly reconstructed. Visitors to the excavation site under the Palazzo Martinengo opposite will discover a fascinating cross-section of the settlement's history spanning some 3000 years. The **Museo di Santa Giulia**, a few buildings away, also takes you far back into the history of Brescia. The Benedictine convent San-Salvatore-Santa-Giulia was founded in 753 by Desiderius, the last king of the Lombards, and built on the site of a Roman villa. The present complex incorporates the medieval church of San Salvatore, the Roman house of worship Santa Maria in Solario, Santa Giulia from the 16th century and the cloister also from this period. The exhibits tracing the long history of the city are presented in a contemporary and fitting way in this impressive setting. In the breathtakingly beautiful **Santa Maria in Solario**

The Piazza della Loggia with its arcades and clock tower (Torre dell' Orologio) is quite clearly modelled on Venetian architecture

The New Cathedral (top left), on the eastern side of the square, is named after Pope Paul VI (1963–78). The real jewel, however, is the Old Cathedral, also known as the 'Rotonda' (top right)

(12th century), with its colourful frescos and brilliant blue starry cupola, a delicate ivory reliquary from the 4th century and the Desiderius Cross (8th/9th centuries) encrusted with precious stones, are perfectly displayed.

From the 15th century onwards Brescia enjoyed an economic boom under Venetian rule. The representative buildings on the **Piazza della Loggia** testify to this – first and foremost the loggia itself, begun in 1492 and completed in the 16th century by the Venetian architects Jacopo Sansovino and Andrea Palladio. Its roof, however, was lost in a fire and a somewhat clumsy replacement added in 1914. On the south side of the *piazza* are the Monte di Pietà, the former municipal pawn office (15th century) and its more modern counterpart, Monte Nuovo. The twin-arched Renaissance building in between has a row of delicate window openings above. The three-arched loggia opposite supports the **Torre dell'Orologio**, crowned by two figures which strike the clock's bell. The Viscontis built a fortress in the 15th century on the hill, Cidneo, named after a mythical Ligurian god. It now houses an arms museum as well as the **Museo del Risorgimento**, documenting the fight for independence. The medieval market district was pulled down in the 1920s and '30s

THE 'LONG BEARDS': LONGOBARDS IN LOMBARDY

During the Migration Period, the Lombards or Longobards – a Germanic tribe from the north – pushed south into the region in Italy that still bears their name. According to legend, 'Longobard' derives from the 'long beards' that they tied around the chins of their womenfolk so that they looked like men and could enter a battlefield. However, it is more probable that the name comes from a long-handled axe, similar to a halberd. Seven 'Places of Power' where the Lombards erected important buildings – fortresses, churches and monasteries – have been combined to form one UNESCO World Heritage Site: Benevento, Brescia, Campello sul Clitunno, Castelseprio, Cividale del Friuli, Monte Sant'Angelo and Spoleto.

to make way for the monumental **Piazza della Vittoria**. The architect was Marcello Piacentini, a precursor of the *razionalismo* style. Il Duce himself inaugurated the *piazza* in 1932.

Worldly and ecclesiastic powers rub shoulders on the rectangular **Piazza Paolo VI**. The **Broletto**, the town hall, combines architectural elements from the 12th to the 18th centuries. The **Duomo Nuovo** next door has a richly subdivided Baroque and Classicist façade as well as the highest dome in Italy. The brick façade of the **Duomo Vecchio** by comparison is totally in-conspicuous. Built in the 12th century, it comprises two cylindrical sections. Inside, steps lead down to the level of the previous building on the site, an Early Christian basilica with fragments of a mosaic preserved behind glass. The exquisite treasury – the Tesoro delle Sante Croci, that includes two reliquary crosses (14th/15th centuries) – is housed in a side chapel.

The Tempio Capitolino, built in 78AD, is on the narrow northern side of the Ancient Roman forum

TAKING A BREAK

Coffea di Nevola Ivan, at Corso Zanardelli 26, serves excellent coffee and hot chocolate. For something more substantial try **Raffa** at no. 15 in Corso Magenta nearby.

✚ 179 D1/E2

Capitolium
✉ Via Musei 55 ☎ www.bresciamusei.com ⏱ Oct–Feb Fri–Sun 105; March–15 June Tue–Sun 10–5, 16 June–Sep Tue–Sun 11–7 💷 €4

Museo di Santa Giulia
✉ Via Musei 81b ☎ www.bresciamusei.com
⏱ Oct–15 June Tue–Sun 9:30–5:30, 16 June–Sep Tue–Sun 10:30–7
💷 €10

Museo del Risorgimento
✉ Via Castello 9 ☎ www.bresciamusei.com
⏱ Oct–15 June Thu–Sun 10–5, 16 June–Sep Fri–Sun 11–7
💷 €5

INSIDER INFO

- Try to **arrive early** and find a space in one of the **big car parks** near Corso Zanardelli (the one on the Piazza Vittoria is well signed) so as to be close to the tourist office and the main sights.
- The fruit and vegetable market on the Piazza del Mercato is held every day; the bigger **weekly market** on Saturdays on the Piazza della Loggia.

At Your Leisure

44 Boario Terme

Boario is named after the natural hot water that is now piped to the Thermal Establishment, a fine building set among gardens and parkland against a backdrop of high mountains. The spa owes its fame to the alchemist Paracelsus (1493–1541) who praised the healing power of the water. Close to Boario, in the **Parco delle Luine**, some of the rock drawings for which the Val Camonica is renowned can be seen. Alternatively, follow the road into the Val di Scalve, going through Angolo Terme, a small spa village. From here a narrow road reaches the deep-blue **Lago Moro**, while the main road cuts through the Dezzo Gorge with good views of the Orobie Alps.
➕ 179 D4

Parco delle Luine
☎ 0364 54 11 00
🕐 Tue–Sun 9–noon, 2–5 🎫 Free

45 Breno

From Boario Terme the road through the Val Camonica heads towards Breno, but a short detour leads to Ésine, where the 14th-century church of **Santa Maria Assunta**

Idyllic countryside: the Val Camonica (here with a view of Breno Castle)

Northern Lombardy

Marvels from the past: prehistoric rock drawings in the Parco Nazionale delle Incisioni Rupestri

is a National Monument, famous for its *campanile* and 15th-century frescoes. A 14th-century castle on a rocky outcrop towers over Breno. The town's museum focuses on local history.

✚ 179 E5

Castello
☎ 0364 2 29 70 🕐 Daily 9am–10pm 💶 Free

Museo Camuno
☎ 0364 32 40 99 🕐 Mon, Wed, Thu 9–noon, Tue, Sat 9–noon, 3–6, Fri, Sun 3–6 💶 €4

46 Capo di Ponte

The Camuni, an ancient alpine people who created the rock drawings in Val Camonica that is now a UNESCO World Heritage Site, settled in the valley in the Middle Paleolithic period and left a huge number of symbols and images. The oldest of the more

than 200,000 individual engravings have been dated to around 6000 BC. There are all sorts of differnt motifs. A large number of pictures are of the animals they hunted, especially stags. Images of armed riders are equally predominant. Many of the drawings are difficult for us to interpret today. At Capo di Ponte, about 12km (7mi) north of Breno, there is a museum on the drawings together with a study centre. Five easy trails lead visitors to the most attractive rocks with information boards. To see everything, allow four hours. The nearby **Museo Didatico d'Arte e Vita Preistorico** has a reconstructed Camuni village.

✚ 179 F5

Centro Camuno di Studi Preistorico
✉ Via Marconi 7, Capo di Ponte
☎ 0364 4 20 91 🕐 Mon–Fri 9–5 💶 Free

Parco Nazionale delle Incisioni Rupestri
✉ Park next to the Chiesa Delle Sante in the village and follow the waymarked path into the park
☎ 0364 4 21 40
🕐 Tue–Sun 8:30–1:30 💶 €4

Museo Didatico d'Arte e Vita Preistorico
✉ Via Pieve San Siro 4, Capo di Ponte
☎ 0364 4 21 48 🕐 Daily 9–noon, 2–5:30 💶 Free

Where to…
Stay

Prices
Expect to pay per double room, per night
€ under €80   €€ €80–€130   €€€ over €130

BERGAMO

Agnello d'Oro €€
This building in the upper town dates from the late 16th century. Some bedrooms overlook the small square in front. Simply furnished but comfortable rooms.
✚ 178 A3 ✉ Via Gombito 22
☎ 035 24 98 83; www.agnellodoro.it

Cappello d'Oro €€€
A Best Western Premier hotel at the heart of the lower town. The bedrooms are relatively small but well decorated and furnished. Private car park and an excellent restaurant.
✚ 178 A3 ✉ Viale Papa Giovanni XXIII
☎ 035 2 28 90 11;
www.bwhotelcappellodoro-bg.it

Città dei Mille €
An inexpensive hotel on the road to the *autostrada*, but about a 30-minute walk – or a bus ride – from the centre of the lower town. Each floor is a different colour; includes Garibaldi memorabilia and other curiosities.
✚ 178 A3 ✉ Via Autostrada 3c
☎ 035 31 74 00; www.cittadiemille.it

Excelsior San Marco €€€
Midway between the funicular to the upper town and the centre of the lower town. Spacious rooms, some with a view of the upper town. The hotel restaurant (Colonna) is one of the best in the city. Private car park.
✚ 178 A3 ✉ Piazza della Repubblica 6
☎ 035 36 61 11; www.hotelsanmarco.com

BOARIO TERME

Rizzi €€€
One of the best hotels in a spa town where there is a lot of competition. Spacious, well-appointed rooms. The spa itself is just 100m away. Lovely garden and a very good restaurant.
✚ 179 D4 ✉ Via Carducci 11
☎ 0364 53 16 17; www.albergorizzi.it

BRENO

Giardino €
A medium-size hotel with good facilities ideally situated for an exploration of Val Camonica.
✚ 179 E5 ✉ Via 28 Aprile
☎ 0364 32 11 84;
www.cominelli.com/hotelgiardino

BRESCIA

Albergo Orologio €€
This 3-star boutique hotel is just behind the Piazza Loggia. Ask for a room with a view. Care has been taken to blend antique furniture with modern amenities. Very friendly and helpful staff.
✚ 179 D1/E2 ✉ Via Beccaria 17
☎ 030 3 75 54 11; www.albergoorologio.it

Trento €
This small hotel is within walking distance of all the main visitor sights and the shopping centre. Pleasant rooms, a good restaurant and friendly staff.
✚ 179 D1/E2
✉ Piazza Cesare Battisti 27–29
☎ 030 38 07 68

Where to...
Eat and Drink

Prices

Expect to pay for a three-course meal for one, excluding drinks and service

€ under €30   € €30–€60   €€€ over €60

BERGAMO

Airoldi €

A solid option for a light lunch, dinner or drinks in the lower town. The menu on a blackboard includes steaks and pasta dishes.

🗺 178 A3 ✉ Viale Papa Giovanni XXIII 18 ☎ 035 24 44 23 🕐 Mon–Sat 7 am–11 pm

Borgo €€

Lively, colourful *osteria* packed with locals enjoying good home cooking. Pizzas are baked in a wood-burning oven and a more extensive menu for €25 is offered in the evening.

🗺 178 A3 ✉ Via San Lazzaro 8 ☎ 035 24 24 52 🕐 Closed Sun

La Bruschetta €€

A beautiful building with vaulted stone ceilings. Fish and meat dishes and an excellent range of pizzas.

🗺 178 A3 ✉ Via G d'Alzano 1 ☎ 035 22 12 65 🕐 Closed Mon. Dinner only

Colleoni & Dell'Angelo €€€

Housed in a medieval *palazzo* with vaulted ceilings and frescoed walls. The Bergamesque ravioli with butter and sage is hard to beat. An all-inclusive menu for €50 is sometimes available.

🗺 178 A3 ✉ Piazza Vecchia 7 ☎ 035 23 25 96 🕐 Closed Mon and for two weeks in Aug

Da Ornella €€

Lovely little place in the Old Town specialising in polenta served with meat in cast-iron bowls. Also *polenta taragna* (cooked with butter and cheese) and rabbit.

🗺 178 A3 ✉ Via Gombito 15 ☎ 035 23 27 36 🕐 Closed Thu and Fri lunch

BOARIO TERME

Airone €   *Insider Tip*

The *pizzocheri* – a speciality from the Lombard region made of buckwheat and wheat flour – and polenta, and a beef stew with mushrooms and cream, are highlights on the menu, but there is much else to enjoy in this charming restaurant.

🗺 179 D4 ✉ Via Nazionale 15 ☎ 0364 53 12 76

BRESCIA

Al Teatro €

Excellent pizzeria close to the city centre. Good menu and value-for-money pizzas.

🗺 179 D1/E2 ✉ Via Mazzini 36 ☎ 030 4 42 51

Castello Malvezzi €€

Elegant building with a palatial atmosphere. Traditional dishes with a twist, delicious!

🗺 179 D1/E2 ✉ Via Colle San Giuseppe ☎ 030 2 00 42 24 🕐 Closed Mon and Tue. Dinner only Wed–Fri

La Sosta €€

A marvellous restaurant in the stables of the Palazzo Martinengo. Brescian specialities such as goat are on the menu. Booking in advance is advised.

🗺 179 D1/E2 ✉ Via San Martino della Battaglia 20 ☎ 030 29 56 03 🕐 Closed Mon and Sun eve

Where to…
Shop

As major cities, both Brescia and Bergamo have large shopping areas and some out-of-town centres. Many international brands have outlets in the two towns but there are also lots of individual shops too.

BRESCIA

For jewellery, the following are certainly worth a look: **Giarin** (Via San Martino della Battaglia), try **Ghidini**, (Corso Magenta 8b) for unusual, exciting designs and **Emozioni d'Oro**, (Via Valcamonica 17). For shoes try **Fratelli Rossetti** (Corso Zanardelli 1) and **Romano** (Corso Palestro13).

Many designer fabrics can be found at **Casa Sovrana** in Portici X Giornate.

And for antiques look out for **Cronos**, Galleria al Duomo (Via X Giornate), **Ceralacca** (Via Fratelli Porcellana 42), **Antic Oro** (Vicolo della Speranza 3d), for both old and new jewellery and **Rino Fossati** (Via Beccaria 3a).

The biggest department store in the city centre is **Coin** at the corner of Corso Magenta and Via San Martino della Battaglia. The huge out-of-town **Franciacorta Outlet Village** is on the Bergamo road, at the 'Ospitaletto' exit on the A4. There are some 160 shops of internationally well-known brands from Adidas to Timberland, providing a massive selection at low prices with something for everyone. And if you fancy a break while shopping, there are around a dozen bars and restaurants to quench your thirst and satisfy your hunger. Open daily until 20, Sat and Sun 21, Mon opens at 14:30, otherwise at 10 (www.franciacortaoutlet.it).

BERGAMO CITTÀ BASSA

There are many boutiques for ladies' fashions in Via XX Septembre. **La Perla** (Sentierone 40) has high-quality swimwear and underclothes.

For shoes look for **Pompeo** (Via XX Septembre 27), **Bruschi** (Via XX Septembre 39), **Fratelli Rossetti** (Via XX Septembre 52) and **Dev** (Via XX Septembre 85–87).

For handbags and other leather goods there is **Diana** (Via XX Septembre 40).

The area around the **Accademia Carrara** is popular with artists and there are several studios, most notably that of Sergio Garau (Via San Tomaso 88a), who paints on old wood and cloth. Close to Sergio's studio there is a good antique shop – **GLA Antichità** (Via Sant'Orsola 17).

The biggest department store in the city centre is **Coin** (Largo Medaglie d'Oro, Via Zambonate 11).

BERGAMO CITTÀ ALTA

The upper town is both much smaller and much more given over to outlets for visitors with its restaurants, bars, etc. But there are some gems, including **Babilonia** (Via Gombito 12d) which sells chic ladies' clothing. Opposite the restaurant Colleoni on the Piazza Vecchia is **Daniela Gregis** who designs and makes one-off articles and has already been featured in Vogue.

For menswear **Franco Loda** (Via Gombito 17) is excellent, whereas **Cesare Albert** (Via Bartolomeo Colleoni 5b) is the place to go for some of the best children's clothes in the area.

Brivio (Via B Colleoni 19a) has excellent jewellery and silverware. For gifts, the candles at **RR Candele** (Via B Colleoni 15m) are good value.

🏠 **Cooperativa Libraria II Quarttiere** (Via Gombito 24a) is a well-stocked stationers with a good range of toys as well.

Insider Tip

Where to...
Go Out

WALKING

Both Bergamo and Brescia are excellent centres from which to explore the valleys that head north towards the Alps. North of Bergamo are the **Val Brembana** and **Val Seriana**. Val Seriana is famous for the Cascata del Serio.

North of Brescia, there is lovely countryside and good walking in **Val Camonica**, famous for its rock drawings, **Val Sabbia** and **Val Trompia**, as well as in the **Franciacorta,** northwest of the city.

GOLF

There are several golf courses in the area close to Bergamo and Brescia. **Francaciorta Golf Club** has an unusual 'Wine Golf Course' (www.franciacortagolfclub.com), with each of the 9 holes having names such as 'Brut', 'Saten' and 'Rosé'.

OTHER SPORTS

There are opportunities for tennis, squash, etc. in the sports centres in each of the cities. From Brescia, the watersports facilities on the western side of Lake Garda can be easily reached.

THEATRE AND CINEMA

There are cinemas in Brescia and Bergamo. At **Manerbio** – just off the A21 *autostrada* south of Brescia – there is a multi-screen cinema.

The **Donizetti Theatre** in Bergamo has four seasons each year. The opera season is from September to December, the drama season from November to April. There is a jazz festival in February and a season of dance/ballet from January to April.

The **Teatro Grande** in Brescia has an opera season from September to November, a drama season from November to April and a season of concerts from October to March.

Brescia also has two other theatres, **Teatro di Santa Chiara** and **Teatro Sancarlino**.

NIGHTLIFE

In Bergamo there are discos in Via San Lorenzo (**Dell'Angelo**) and Via Bascensis (the **Ritmo**). There are also around a dozen discos and nightclubs in Brescia. At present the popular ones are **Orange Blue** (146 Via Mandolossa), **Circus** (127 Via Dalmazia), and **Fura** (Via Lavagrome 13, Lonato).

FESTIVALS

Brescia hosts an international **piano festival** (held jointly with Bergamo) from April to June and a series of organ concerts from mid-September to mid-October in its churches.

Most famous of all is the **Mille Miglia** (► 125) car race which, starting in Brescia, was held annually until 1957, when it was stopped after a series of accidents involving the deaths of spectators. In 1977 the event was revived as a three-day veteran car rally held in May, running from Brescia to Ferrara, then to Rome and back to Brescia.

MARKETS

There is an **antiques market** on the Piazza Cittadella in Bergamo's Città Alta on the third Sunday of the month. There is also a **book fair** at the Sentierone in April and May.

Excursions

Excursions

There are lots of lovely excursions to be had both from Lake Garda and Verona. Cremona to the south of Brescia, Mantua (Mantova) to the south of Verona and Vicenza, to the northeast of the city on the Adige are all interesting and easy to reach. Each of these towns has its own character and is well worth a visit.

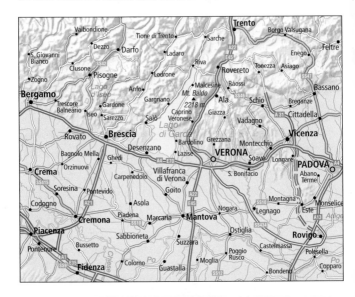

Cremona

Two pleasures for the senses made Cremona famous. One is the magical music made on a Cremona violin, known the world over; the other is *torrone* – that sweet nougat speciality that was reputedly first made for a royal wedding in 1441. Both are still available today – and are there to be enjoyed!

Cremona's *centro storico* around the Piazza del Comune, with its cathedral and the Torrazzo clock tower, testifies to its history from the Communal Period to the peak of the Renaissance

The first violin workshop was founded in the 16th century by the patrician family Amati; this was followed by those of the families Guarneri and Stradivari. Today, there is still a famous violin-makers' school and a number of workshops. What is perhaps less well-known than its musical heritage is that Cremona has several architectural highlights to offer too which make a visit a must.

Left: Exquisite types of wood and unsurpassed sound – music is in the air in and around Cremona

The centre of the Old Town is the Piazza del Comune with the baptistry, cathedral, the Palazzo del Comune and the Loggia dei Militi. This is where the city's landmark clock tower, the **Torrazzo**, is located. Built in the mid-13th century it is the tallest in Italy at a height of 111m (364ft). The large Renaissance clock is on the west façade and, apart from showing the time and date, it also used to provide astronomical information. The

Excursions

Torrazzo is linked to the cathedral by the elegant Portico della Bertazzola. Building work started in the Lombard-Romanesque style in 1107 and it was completed in the Gothic style in 1332. The interior is decorated with 16th-century frescos by notable artists from Lombardy. The baptistry (1167) next to the cathedral has an octagonal ground plan and a font by Lorenzo Trotti from the first half of the 16th century.

The most famous violins made in local workshops are exhibited in the **Palazzo Comunale**. These include the small *Il Cremonese* of 1715 by Antonio Stradivari, *L'Hammerle* of 1658 by Nicolò Amati and a violin by Giuseppe Antonio Guarneri of 1734 once played by the Israeli violinist Pinchas Zukerman. The Palazzo Affaitati (16th century) is reached by crossing the busy Corso Campi. It houses the **Museo Civico** 'Ala Ponzone' with works by local artists from the 16th century. The Stradivari Museum is dedicated to the city's most famous violin maker. There are several modern violin workshops in the vicinity. To the north of the Piazza del Commune is Stradivari's tomb made of red marble.

San Sigismondo

Take a 20-minute walk east of the *palazzo* or a ride on bus no. 2. San Sigismondo, on the Casalmaggiore road, is where Franceso Sforza married Bianca Visconti, a union that increased the prosperity of Cremona. The present church with beautiful frescos was built in 1463 to commemorate the marriage and replaced an older building.

TAKING A BREAK

Try **Pasticceria Duomo** at 6 Via Bocaccino, near the cathedral, for coffee and pastries.

➕ 178 off C1

Torrazzo
☎ 0372 49 50 29 🕐 Daily 10–1, 2:30–6 💶 €5

Palazzo Comunale
☎ 0372 40 72 69 🕐 Mon–Sat 9–6, Sun 10–5 💶 Free

Museo Civico
☎ 0372 40 77 70 🕐 Tue–Sat 9–6, Sun 10–6 💶 €7

INSIDER INFO

Insider Tip

- A recording of the sound produced by the most famous violins is played in the **Saletta dei Violini**. These can also be played live on request.
- Opera fans will not want to miss seeing **the house where Verdi was born** in Roncole, a suburb of Busseto, some 30k (18m) southeast of Cremona.

Mantova

South of Peschiera del Garda, the river that flows out of Lake Garda, the Mincio, runs into low-lying, swampy ground. Here it languidly turns right, forming three lagoons. Alone the town's situation on the lake is impressive. On top of this are the well-preserved historical buildings and squares. Gourmands also come in for a treat here – the majority of the famous Parma ham comes from this area.

Mantua's numerous artistic treasures date largely from after 1328 when the town was ruled for 300 years by the Gonzaga family of nobles. Famous architects such as Leon Battista Alberti and, later, Raphael's pupil Giulio Romano were called to Mantua. Antonio Pisanello, Andrea Mantegna and Peter Paul Rubens all worked as court painters and Claudio Monteverdi was a musician at the Gonzaga court. In 70 BC, the poet Virgil was born in the Ancient Roman village of Andes, now Pietole, nearby. This stretch of land was named Virgilio in his honour. In 1707 the Austrian Habsburgs assumed control until 1866. Verdi's opera *Rigoletto* is set in Mantua and, in Shakespeare's *Romeo and Juliet*, the hero is banned to this town.

Palazzo Ducale

If you have driven south along the A22 from Verona and taken the Mantova North exit, you will enter the city along Via Legnago, crossing a bridge between the Lago di Mezzo (on the right) and the Lago Inferiore (on the left). Here, on the eastern side of the **Piazza Sordello**, is the town's most magnificent building – Italy's largest palace complex

The medieval Piazza delle Erbe is lit up at nightfall

Excursions

after the Vatican and, at one time, one of the most richly furnished residences in Europe. The individual buildings that make up the **Palazzo Ducale** were erected between the 13th and 17th centuries. From the outside, the enormous size of the Gonzaga palace can only be imagined. The complex, that is virtually a town within a town, is entered via a small gateway. The palace covers a total area of 34,000m² (366,000ft²) and comprises eight main buildings with more than 500 rooms as well as 15 separate gardens and inner courtyards. Only a small part of this complex, however, is open to the public. One of the main sights is the Camera degli Sposi, painted by Andrea Mantegna in 1465–74. This 'bridal suite' is in the form of a pavilion with portraits of members of the Gonzaga family lining the walls. In the middle of the domed ceiling is a round opening that reveals the painted heavens beyond. Mantegna's illusionist style was to have a great influence on the painting and architectural designs of his contemporaries.

The two-storey **Rotonda di San Lorenzo**, one of the most important Romanesque buildings in Lombardy, is in the southeastern corner of the **Piazza delle Erbe.** The Palazzo della Ragione, the former town hall dating from 1250 is on the north side. Opposite is the **Basilica Sant'Andrea**, built from 1472 onwards to a design by Leon Battista Alberti. It is considered the first Renaissance building in Lombardy. The tomb of Andrea Mantegna, who died in Mantua in 1506, is in the first side chapel on the left. The bust of the artist – which is thought to be a self-portrait – is rightly famous.

The **Palazzo del Te** is the magnus opus of Giulio Romano, Federico II's favourite architect, and was built by the art-loving duke in 1525–35 on the island of Te which, until the lake was drained in the 18th century, could only be reached across a bridge.

TAKING A BREAK

Mantova is famous for its traditional cuisine, including *stracotto di asino* (donkey stew) and a garlic salami that will make your eyes water. Try the former at **Due Cavallini**, at Via Salnitro 5. The latter is best purchased and eaten in private: try **Panificio Freddi** at Piazza Cavallotti 7.

Insider Tip

✚ 180 off C1

Palazzo Ducale
☎ 0376 35 21 00
🕐 Tue–Sun 8:15–7:15 (last ticket 6:20) 💶 €6.50

Basilica Sant'Andrea
🕐 Daily 8–noon, 3–7 💶 Free

Palazzo del Te
☎ 0376 32 32 66 🕐 Mon 1–6, Tue–Sun 9–6 💶 €13

Vicenza

This city largely owes its fame to Andrea Palladio, the last great Renaissance architect who wrote architectural history with his villas and whose buildings in Vicenza, as well as in the region of Veneto as a whole, are now UNESCO World Heritage Sites.

Palladio's most important early work can be found on the long-drawn out Piazza dei Signori that has been the centre of public and private life in the city since Roman times. The **Palazzo della Ragione** – often called the Basilica Palladion (not open to the public at present) – gave the architect with his breakthrough. Palladio was the winner of a competition to improve the building. He encased the core with a two-storey marble portico supported on columns. A statue of Palladio (1859) is on the southwest side of the basilica. Opposite the basilica is the Palazzo del Monte di Pietà, the former municipal pawn office (15th century) that flanks the Baroque façade of the church of San Vicenzo (1617) on both sides. On the north side of the *piazza* is the **Loggia del Capitanio**, the seat of the Venetian governor of Vicenza, begun in 1571 by Palladio. Having changed hands several times in the 14th century, it passed to the Republic of Venice in 1404, under whose rule the city experienced its heyday.

To the northwest of the Piazza dei Signori is the Corso Andrea Palladio – the city's perfectly straight main thoroughfare lined with palaces. The Corso leads in the Piazza Castello which has boasts a Scaliger tower. To the left, on the short side of the square, is the Palazzo Porto-Breganze. Designed by Palladio it was executed by Vincenzo Scamozzi around 1600 and displays the heavy columns typical of Palladio's late work. The **Pinacoteca Civica**, the municipal art collection at the northeast end of the Corso Andrea Palladio, is housed in the Palazzo Chiericati

Vicenza's Piazza dei Signori extends over the site of the former Roman forum

(1551–57) that is also considered one of Palladio's principal works. The collection includes works by Venetian painters from the Middle Ages to Mannerism, including paintings by Tiepolo and Piazzetto. One of Palladio's most beautiful buildings and, at the same time, his last, is the **Teatro Olimpico**, the first free-standing theatre with a roof and an auditorium in the shape of an amphitheatre. Concerts are now held here. One of the most beautiful of Palladio's villas, **La Rotonda**, is open to the public. It is located on the southern edge of the city, less than 3km (1.8mi) from the Teatro Olimpico.

Palladio has been attested as having the best possible taste, reflected in the proportions and symmetry of his works. The Villa Rotonda near Vicenza is a UNESCO World Heritage Site

TAKING A BREAK

There are good cafés and cake shops near the Piazza dei Signori as well as restaurants selling specialities such as polenta (try it grilled) and salted cod.

✚ 181 off F2

Pinacoteca Civica
✉ Palazzo Chiericati ☎ 0444 22 28 11 🕐 Tue–Sun 9–5 💶 €10

Teatro Olimpico
✉ Piazza Matteotti 11 ☎ 0444 22 28 00; www.teatrolimpicovicenza.it
🕐 Tue–Sun 9–4:30 💶 €8.50

La Rotonda
✉ Via della Rotonda 45 ☎ 0444 22 28 00 🕐 Mid-March–Oct Tue–Sun 10–noon, 3–6, until 5 rest of the year (in winter generally only to be viewed from the outside)
💶 €5, with a tour of the interior (reservations must be made via e-mail two weeks in advance to: prenotazioni@villalarotonda.it) €10

INSIDER INFO

- A **combined entrance ticket, the Vicenza Card,** is available for all the city's main attractions.
- If the **Palladio villas** are your main interest, do not come in winter as most of them are shut from November to March.
- Vicenza is a centre for Italian **gold-working**, with many craft studios.

Walks & Tours

1 MONTE BALDO
Walk

DISTANCE 8km (5mi)   **TIME** 2.5 hours
START/END POINT Lower cable-car station,
Malcesine (tel: 045 7 40 02 06) ✚ 181 D4

Walkers on their way to the viewpoint on Monte Baldo

This exhilarating walk is through beautiful mountain scenery where a lot of endemic flora and fauna can be seen as well as panoramic views of the lake. Take a rain and windproof jacket as the temperature on the ridge will be cooler than at the lakeside and thunderstorms can brew up quickly on the ridge. The walk can be extended by continuing to the highest point on the Monte Baldo ridge, but this involves rugged terrain and should only be attempted by experienced hillwalkers.

❶–❷
Take the cable-car to the summit of Monte Baldo.

❷–❸
Leave the cable-car and turn right, descending briefly (past a café) to reach an electricity sub-station and a path junction. Go straight ahead towards the ski-lift.

360° PANORAMA ON THE WAY UP
The 4.3km (2.7mi) trip to the top of the mountain takes just ten minutes. En route, the cabins of the 'Funivia Malcesine – Monte Baldo' – one of the most modern cable-cars in the world – rotate slowly through 360 degrees before the summit is reached at 2000m (6562ft). Check the timetable and prices on arrival or under www.funiviedelbaldo.it. At present, during the summer season, the cable-car operates every day from April until October, every 30 minutes between 8 and 18:00. The last descent is at 18:45. Price: €20 (return).

3–4

Keep to the right of the ski lift and follow the marked route 651 as it climbs over rough, then much gentler, terrain to a chair lift.

4–5

The end point of the shorter walk is now in sight. Go through the fence into the nature reserve and follow the clear path along the ridge studded with dwarf-pines. The grassy terrain gradually gives way to rougher ground but the going is never very arduous and the path is always obvious.

The objective of the short walk, Cima delle Pozzette, at 2132m (6972ft), is reached after about 1.5 hours' walking. On a clear day the view is breathtaking, extending west to Monte Rosa, taking in the Adamello and the Alps north of it, and east as far as the Julian Alps. Inevitably, however, the eye is

selves about weather conditions before setting out.

5–6

Route 651 continues straight-forwardly from Cima delle Pozzette, dropping down almost 200m (654ft) then rising towards the summit of Cima del Longino (2179m/7096ft). From here the path becomes more rugged and spectacular, going over Cima Val Finestra (2084m/6815ft) then edging east around the cliffs of Cima Valdritta. It now becomes a true mountain path, experience and sure-footedness being required to follow the northern ridge to the summit of Cima Valdritta (2218m/7253ft), the highest point of Monte Baldo.

From Cima Valdritta, reverse the route, taking great care on descents, to Cima delle Pozzette and back to the cable-car top station.

drawn to Lake Garda, stretching out below the ridge.

The walk can be extended. This adds 6.5km (4mi) and a further two hours to the walk. The long walk is, therefore, 4.5 hours long, much of it above 2000m (6540ft) and half of it on a very rugged mountain with rescue for injured walkers several hours away. Please be very cautious and inform your-

Walks & Tours

2 SIRMIONE
Walk

DISTANCE 3km (2mi) **TIME** 1 hour
START/END POINT Rocca Scaligera, Sirmione ✚ 180 C2

The peninsula and Old Town of Sirmione form one of the highlights of Lake Garda. This short walk takes in the best the two have to offer, with fine views and historic places along the way.

1–2
From the castle head into the Old Town, soon turning right into Via Dante which is signed for the Passeggiata Panoramica. In Via Dante the lake moat surrounding the castle is to your right. Turn left, going slightly uphill – again following a Passeggiata Panoramica sign. Bear right to reach a small garden to your right. Go through the archway in the Old Town wall ahead. Beyond, to your left, is the church of **Santa Maria Maggiore**.

2–3
Go down steps, turn right and down more steps to reach a gravelled area next to the lake. Follow the lakeside path ahead. There are usually black-headed gulls and mallards here as they have become used to being fed by visitors. Stone seats are strategically placed to enjoy both the birds and the view across the lake to Monte Baldo. The path moves away from the lake, passing an area of rushes and tall grasses, with the occasional olive tree, to your right.

3–4
Go past the entrance to the jetty of the Palace Hotel Villa Cortine (strictly private – guests only). The gentle lapping of water on the shore is now the only sound to disrupt the peace.

Sirmione's Scaliger Castle is one of the best-preserved moated fortresses in Europe

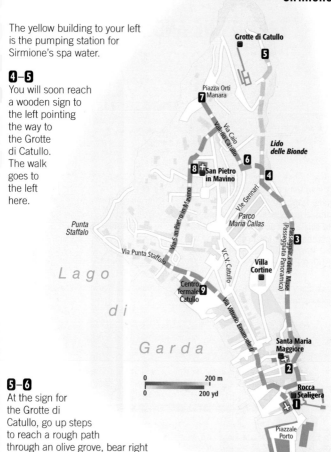

The yellow building to your left is the pumping station for Sirmione's spa water.

4–5

You will soon reach a wooden sign to the left pointing the way to the Grotte di Catullo. The walk goes to the left here.

5–6

At the sign for the Grotte di Catullo, go up steps to reach a rough path through an olive grove, bear right along a path and then take the steps on the left to reach a stepped path.

6–7

At the top of the steps turn right along Via Catullound and follow it as far as the **Piazzale Orti Manara**. There are excellent lake views from here and the **Grotte di Catullo** are to the right.

7–8

Retrace the walk along Via Catullo, but after passing the Hotel Ideal, turn right along a lane signposted San Pietro in Mavino. Follow this uphill through an olive grove, then turn right (still heading towards San Pietro), bearing left to the church.

8–9

Ignore Via Faustina opposite the church and go straight ahead (or turn left from the church). The lane goes downhill, passing the Hotel Villa Maria to the left. At the crossroads turn left outside the Hotel Serenella.

9–1

You are now in Sirmione's main shopping area. Walk through an impressive archway, through another archway and bear left to follow the marble paving back to the castle.

3 TREMOSINE AND TIGNALE
Drive

DISTANCE 45km (28mi)   TIME 2 hours
START POINT Limone sul Garda ✚ 181 C4
END POINT Gargnano ✚ 180 C3

Above the northwestern shore of
Lake Garda lie two high plateaus of
alpine meadows. The road to them
is twisty and occasionally tortuous
but the views of the mountains to
the north, mountain villages and
Lake Garda are breathtaking.

1–2

At the southern end of Limone sul
Garda (➤ 62) is a large car park
used by day visitors to the town.
From here, take the route back to
the Gardesana Occidentale, the
road that follows the western shore

The 'scary terrace' at Hotel Paradiso in Pieve di Tremosine (www.terrazzadelbrivido.it)
juts out several feet over a sheer drop

of the lake and turn left towards the towns on the lake to the south. Ignore the first turn on the right (signed for Tremosine) and go past a sign welcoming you to the district of Tremosine.

2–3

The Gardesana Occidentale now goes through a series of four tunnels. The first two are relatively short (about 100m), the third is longer (about 500m), the fourth about 2.5km (1.5mi). About 100m after exiting from this fourth tunnel, take the road on the right (Via Benaco) signed Tremosine.

3–4

Go through a short tunnel, beyond which the road becomes very narrow, climbing steeply uphill with winding bends and hairpins

to reach a *galleria* (an open-sided tunnel). Beyond this the road widens and offers the first view of the lake to your right. Go through another tunnel, noting the arched roof: beware – if a lorry or bus is coming the other way it will be in the middle of the road. Beyond the tunnel the road becomes single track again with passing places.

4–5

This is a delightful section of road, with a stream in the wooded gorge to your right and a small bridge that diverts another stream over the road to fall as a waterfall beside it. However, the driving requires concentration and skill if you meet oncoming traffic. Patience and goodwill are required by both drivers.

Go over a tiny bridge to reach a section of road carved out of the

Walks & Tours

Just follow the sun: instead of using the car, take an airy trip around the lake on a Vespa

mountain: the gorge here is very narrow. At a sign for the Hotel Paradiso (this really is beautiful country) a bridge appears ahead and above: you will actually cross this soon as the road doubles back on itself to gain height. Just beyond this the La Forra Ristorante is reached – a good place for an early cup of coffee. The most tortuous section of the drive is now over.

5–6

The road now widens and soon you arrive in Pieve. The route bears right here (signed Voltino), but it is worth stopping in the village to visit the Miralago restaurant, a good place for lunch. The restaurant is cantilevered over a stupendous drop above Lake Garda, so the views are amazing, as is the local cuisine. (To reach the Miralago, go into Piazza Fossato and, with the tourist office behind you, walk straight ahead.)

The tourist office has information on the Parco Regional dell'Alto Garda Bresciano, set up to protect the natural scenery of Tremosine and Tignale and the mountains to the north and west. The wildlife of the park includes roe deer, several varieties of frogs and toads, salamanders, the sulphur-yellow Cleopatra butterfly and, in the high hills, the European brown bear, which has recently returned to the area and is being monitored as part of the 'Life Ursus' project, designed to increase its numbers.

6–7

Back on the drive, follow the road towards Voltino, with terrific views of the mountain villages of the Tremosine. Beyond Priezzo where the church dates from the 7th century the road is slightly wider and the countryside more open. Go through a short, single-track tunnel: the road now winds up to the village of Villa. Just outside the village there is a viewpoint from which to admire the terraced village and surrounding country.

7–8

Ignore a turning to the right (for Voltino and Limone), following the road around to the left and into Vesio. The road through the village is cobbled: a short stop is worthwhile as many of the village houses are very pretty and the church of San Bartolomeo, built in 1760, is worth visiting. At the Y-junction beyond the village bear right towards Brescia, Salò and Tignale, descending slightly through high alpine meadows with forested cliffs. At a crossroads – the first you have encountered – go straight ahead (again signed for Brescia, Salò and Tignale). Ahead now is a fine view of contorted rock strata. A 'Caution Deer' sign warns you that this is wild open country: please take care as the next section of road goes steeply downhill and has several hairpin bends.

8–9

Cross a river (the Torrente Campione) and start to ascend, again through a series of hairpins. The road then descends and climbs to reach a sign welcoming you to Tignale. Just beyond this you will have a glimpse

of Lake Garda and the road becomes a double-width carriageway
for the first time. Ignore the road
ahead signed for Tignale, staying
with the 'main' road to reach a
signed turn to the left for the
Eremo di Monte Castello.

9–10

Turn left for the church. The road
to it is single track and becomes
steep. On the steep section the
scored concrete surface suggests
a difficult track in winter: it soon
becomes apparent why, as a sharp
hairpin is followed by a steeper
section that leads to an archway
barely wide enough for a car.
Beyond, park in the steep, gravel
area in front of the **Church of
Madonna di Monte Castello** (►63).

10–11

After admiring the church and the
view from it, retrace your way back
to the main road, looking out for
roadside shrines with frescoes of
the Stations of the Cross that may
have escaped your attention on the
drive up, and turn left. Go through
Gárdola, bearing left (signed Salò/
Riva) and descending, with an
expanding view of the lake: there
are a couple of places on this road
which offer fine views across the
lake to Malcesine, with Monte Baldo
rising above it. Ignore the turning
for Piovere and continue downhill to
rejoin the Gardesana Occidentale.
Turn right and then left to reach
Gargnano, parking in the centre
for a cup of coffee and a snack
at the Bar Azzurra on the Piazza
Zanardelli.

4 NORTH OF RIVA
Drive

DISTANCE 70km (43mi)   **TIME** 2.5 hours
START/END POINT Porta San Michele, Riva del Garda ✚ 181 D5

North of Riva lie the huge, spiky, rocky peaks of the Brenta Dolomites. On this drive you will be able to enjoy the craggy scenery that has made the Brenta region so famous, but still be back in time for dinner.

❶–❷
At Porta San Michele turn left on to Viale Dante, then right on to Viale Prati. At the stop sign turn right along Viale Giuseppe Canella. Now at the roundabout (Largo Marconi) take the second exit, signposted Varone/Tenno (Via dei Tigli). Bear right, then left, following signs for the Cascata del Varone.

❷–❸
Keep ahead along the road as it bears left, with a view ahead of magnificent rock faces and mountains and a small vineyard on your left. You now start climbing and will soon see the entrance to the **Cascata del Varone** on your left (► 87). There is a picnic area and café here, but it is probably too early in the drive unless you are planning to view the falls.

❸–❹
Continue through Gavazzo, a picturesque village of old houses with shutters and colourful window boxes, going steeply uphill. There is now an expanding view towards Riva and the lake, with occasional parking places to take full advantage of it. The road ahead climbs through several hairpin bends, with olive trees and vines to your left

and right, and the occasional orange tree as well.

❹–❺
Go through Cologna, with its beautiful church and *campanile*. Just beyond the village there is a viewpoint to your right: from here you can see Monte Baldo and the northern lake as well as more local views. The hillside is terraced for olive trees and vines, the terraces held back by impressive walling. There is another picnic area on the right just before reaching Tenno.

At Tenno the old castle is now the Ristorante Castello, an amazing place to have lunch. Beyond, the hairpin bends continue, as do the marvellous views of the mountains either side and the occasional view of the lake.

❺–❻
Go through Ville del Monte, a lovely mixture of Italian and Tyrolean architecture, the roofs having the familiar semi-circular tiles which appear to have been thrown into position. The church here has a lovely *campanile*.

Beyond, Lago di Tenno lies below to your right. Depending upon the weather the lake appears emerald green or turquoise blue – but at all times it is extremely picturesque. After a short descent through woodland you start to ascend again, the architecture now having a Tyrolean feel, although a frescoed church is a

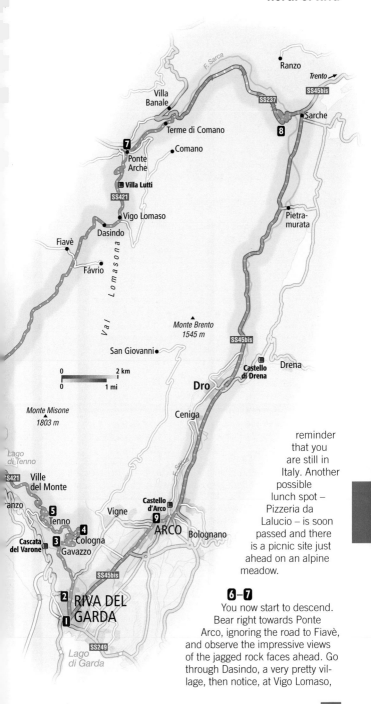

reminder that you are still in Italy. Another possible lunch spot – Pizzeria da Lalucio – is soon passed and there is a picnic site just ahead on an alpine meadow.

6–7

You now start to descend. Bear right towards Ponte Arco, ignoring the road to Fiavè, and observe the impressive views of the jagged rock faces ahead. Go through Dasindo, a very pretty village, then notice, at Vigo Lomaso,

Walks & Tours

Alpine farmsteads are perched just below the tree line

that there are 'Caution Deer' signs. It would add another dimension to the drive to see one, but they are elusive creatures.

Go past the beautiful Villa Lutti, with its curious round tower, and descend steeply through several hairpin bends to reach Ponte Arco. Turn right on to the road for Trento. To the left, the Al Pont is an excellent stop for a cup of coffee or a snack.

7–8

Drive through **Terme di Comano** and follow the narrow, winding road past overhanging cliffs to the right with the Sarca river to the left. On the next section of road you climb steeply with Dolomite-like rock faces and towering peaks to your left.

Go through a very long tunnel, after which there is a view of the mountains and huge rock faces before plunging into another long tunnel which ends with a *galleria*. There are further tunnels: after the fourth there is a picnic area on the left below impressive cliffs.

As you start to descend into Sarche there is a sign for the Zona del Vino Santo DOC with a list of *cantine* to visit should you wish to extend the drive. Sarche is famous among geologists because of the *marocche*, a remarkable area of

huge boulders – the result of three post-glacial landslides.

8–9

Cross the Sarca and turn right at the T-junction towards Riva del Garda. At the roundabout go straight on towards Arco/Riva, driving through a vast vineyard, left and right, which extends for about 2km (1 mile). Recross the river and look out for the Castello di Drena perched on the hillside to your left. The castle was built by the lords of Arco in the late 12th century to defend the valley. The Arco valley is one of only a handful of readily passable routes through the mountains and the Arco lords had constantly to be prepared to meet invading armies. The castle is open to the public. It houses a museum of local history and is open every day except Monday in summer and at weekends only in winter. Ahead you can now also see the castle at Arco, perched on a pyramid of rock. Bear right, crossing the Sarca again to reach **Arco** (➤ 92). If you are stopping here, turn right after crossing the bridge for the car park.

9–10

At the traffic lights go left towards Riva. Soon you will pass a park with a fountain on your right. At the roundabout go straight ahead towards Riva, passing several garden centres. Go past a sign welcoming you to Riva even though there is still a little way to go to reach the town. Go straight ahead through two sets of traffic lights. You will soon reach the Astoria Park Hotel on your right and, to the left opposite the hotel, is the ultra-modern church of San Josep.

Continue in this direction to reach the roundabout where you turned off to Varone at the start of the drive. From here it is about 1km (0.6 mile) back into Riva.

5 LOCAL VINEYARDS
Drive

> **DISTANCE** 80km (50mi)
> **TIME** 3 hours, but longer if wine outlets are visited and lunch is taken
> **START POINT** Tourist information office, Bardolino ✚ 201 D3
> **END POINT** San Severo/A14 *autostrada*, Bardolino ✚ 201 D3

Close to Lake Garda's southeastern tip grapes are grown that are used to make some of Italy's most famous wines, Bardolino and Valpolicella. There is a Strada del Vino through the Bardolino area, but there is no 'official' route through the Valpolicella area. This is a suggested route that links the two areas, making the most of each. The middle section of the route is passed in both directions, a necessary reversal to get between the two.

❶–❷
Start in **Bardolino**, at the tourist information office on the Gardesana Orientale. From the office, head north (towards Garda), but almost immediately take the first right turn (Via Croce) which is signposted to the **Wine Museum**. Ignore the sign for the Strada del Vino on the right, continuing straight on and passing a sign for Affi with a fine row of trees to your right and a boatyard to your left: the first Bardolino vines are to your left after this. Continue through olive groves, soon passing Costadoro, a Bardolino vineyard and then Frantoio where local olive oil can be bought, with good views of the mountains ahead.

Hand-picking the grapes at Lazise in the Bardolino wine-growing area

Walks & Tours

2–3

At the roundabout go straight across (on the road signposted Affi), passing the Naiano vineyard. Wine can be bought in the yellow building. At the next roundabout turn right, passing the La Canova winery on the right. Soon after, bear left along a road signed for Modena/Brennero A22 and Piovezzano, passing through olive groves to reach a little lake on the right. Cross over the A22 *autostrada* and pass the Effegi and Goretex factories to the left.

3–4

At the stop sign turn left towards Sant' Ambrogio di Valpolicella, looking out for the fascinating boulders. Now, at the T-junction turn left, downhill, with good views of the mountains ahead and Monte Baldo to the left. Go past the Stone Gallery, on the right, with its gigantic pieces of stone. The Valpolicella quarries produced the *rossa di Verona* marble from which many of the buildings in the city were constructed. Continue through the pretty village of Sega, then bear right towards the road

(12) and go over the Adige River. Pine trees, cliffs and rock faces are now ahead of you and the Lanza marble works are on your left.

4–5

At the T-junction turn right and drive through Domegliara. At the crossroads take the road left signed Sant'Ambrogio and Negrar and after about 100m (go under a railway bridge and slightly uphill) turn right towards Negrar/San Pietro in Cariano.

Continue uphill, with lovely houses to your left and good views. Go straight ahead at the traffic lights and under a bridge. Your first Valpolicella vineyard is to your right with terraced vineyards to your left. Go under another bridge. There are excellent views of Monte Baldo from this section of road.

5–6

Go straight ahead at the roundabout (signed San Pietro in Cariano/Pedemonte) and again at the traffic lights. Do not bear left with the road but keep going ahead (leaving the main road) past the Famila

supermarket on your right, with more vineyards to both left and right. The road narrows just before a stop sign: turn right at the traffic lights following the sign for Negrar. After passing shops, turn left at the traffic lights. There are beautiful views here, with Monte Baldo on your left and forested hills to your right. The Cantina Sociale on your left is a Valpolicella organisation and sells local wines. Go through Negrar – a pretty village with a picturesque 12th-century church and *campanile* to your left and a river to your right.

6–7

Look out for a left turn signposted Prun/Torbe. The Osteria Nuova Pizzeria, immediately on your right as you turn, is excellent for a short break or for lunch. The road beyond rises steeply through a series of hairpins with excellent views all around. Go through the picturesque village of Torbe and continue uphill. Bear left towards Cerna/Santa Cristina, soon passing incredible marble quarries to the right. The stone has been obtained by excavating into the mountain to form a series of caverns. Long abandoned, the caverns are not pleasant to enter, but the view into them is extraordinary.

7–8

At the stop sign, turn left for Marano di Valpolicella. Soon you pass a picnic area to the left, with stone tables and seats. There are excellent views of woodland here and as the road is usually very quiet this could be an alternative lunch spot. Back on the road, as you descend there are spectacular views to forested mountainside. Continue downhill, passing a lake, through the village of San Rocco with balconied houses and a church with a fine campanile, then through Pezza, with views towards Verona on your left.

A series of downhill hairpin bends takes you to Marano di Valpolicella, with its vast domed church. Go through Prognól and Valgatara, passing the San Rustico and Michele Castellona wine outlets to reach traffic lights at

Walks & Tours

San Floriano. There is a wide selection at the winery Vantini Luigi e Figli, founded in 1908, in the Via Cà dell' Ebreo, as well as guided tours and wine tasting. After all, you can't finish the tour without sampling an Amarone – considered one of Italy's very best red wines.

8–9

Go straight over at the roundabout to retrace your steps through Sant'Ambrogio di Valpolicella. Go straight ahead at the traffic lights (signed Domegliara), with excellent mountain views ahead. At the stop sign turn left (straight ahead is a No Through Road) and at the traffic lights turn right towards Pastrengo.

9–10

At the next traffic lights turn left towards Pastrengo, passing a huge marble works to your right and a sign which marks the end of Valpolicella. Go over a river bridge, then bear left onto a road signed to Pastrengo/Lazise. Go uphill, then bear right towards Lazise.

10–1

Bear left at the Y-junction, heading towards Lazise. Cross the A22 *autostrada*, with you last views of Monte Baldo beyond the conifers on your right. Go past the Bardolino vineyards of Ca' Furia, Podere San Giorgio and Girasole (to your right), then turn left towards Lazise. The Azienda Agricola della Pieve – olive oil sales and an *agriturismo* site – is to your left. Go under a bridge with a little lake on your left, passing through Montiana. This section of the route passes through pleasant country and you soon have your first glimpse of Lake Garda. At the stop sign turn right to reach **Lazise**, following the lakeside road north from there to return to Bardolino.

Delicious wines are maturing in the Barrique barrels at Zeni winery in Bardolino

Practicalities

Practicalities

WHAT YOU NEED

	Some countries require a passport to remain valid for a minimum period (usually at least six months) beyond the date of entry – check beforehand.	UK	USA	Canada	Australia	Ireland	Netherlands	Germany
● Required ○ Suggested ▲ Not required								
Passport/National Identity Card		●	●	●	●	●	●	●
Visa (regulations can change – check before booking)		▲	▲	▲	▲	▲	▲	▲
Onward or Return Ticket		▲	○	○	○	▲	▲	▲
Health Inoculations (tetanus and polio recommended)		▲	▲	▲	▲	▲	▲	▲
Travel Insurance		○	○	○	○	○	○	○
Driving Licence (national)		●	●	●	●	●	●	●
Car Insurance Certificate		●	●	●	●	●	●	●
Car Registration Document		●	●	●	●	●	●	●

WHEN TO GO

High seasaon   Low season

JAN	FEB	MAR	APRIL	MAY	JUNE	JULY	AUG	SEP	OCT	NOV	DEC
5°C	7°C	12°C	17°C	20°C	24°C	27°C	26°C	22°C	16°C	11°C	6°C
41°F	45°F	54°F	63°F	68°F	75°F	81°F	79°F	72°F	61°F	52°F	54°F

☀ Sun   🌧 Wet   🌤 Sunshine & showers   ☁ Cloud

Italy's climate is **predominantly Mediterranean** but, in the north, the proximity of the Alps tempers the heat of summer while the lakes, acting like giant storage radiators, take the edge off the cold of winter. The result is one of the most invigorating climates in Europe – a fact not lost on 19th-century royalty and the aristocracy who visited this area and had villas built.

Summer days can be hot, but are more usually comfortably warm. If the temperature does soar, the breezes generated by the lakes are always there to relieve the heat. In winter there can be rain and fog – and there can also be snow, but this is usually confined to the high ridges and adds skiing to the list of activities the area has to offer.

GETTING ADVANCE INFORMATION

Websites
- Italian Tourist Office for US: www.italiantourism.com
- Bergamo: www.turismo.bergamo.it
- Brescia: www.bresciatourism.it
- Lake Como: www.lakecomo.com
- Lake Garda: www.gardalake.it
- Verona: www.tourism.verona.it

GETTING THERE

By Air Northern Italy has major airports in Turin, Milan and Venice, plus smaller connecting airports across the country. International flights from across Europe also land at smaller airports such as Verona, Bergamo and Brescia.

From the UK, airports are served by Italy's international carrier, Alitalia (tel: 087 14 24 14 24, www.alitalia.co.uk), British Airways (tel: 0 87 08 50 98 50 in UK, 1 99 71 22 66 in Italy, www.ba.com), bmi baby (tel: 0 87 12 24 02 24, www.bmibaby.com), easyJet (tel: 087 17 50 01 00, www.easyjet.com), and Ryanair (tel: 0 87 12 46 00 00, www.ryanair.com). Flying time varies from about 2 to 3.5 hours.

From the US, numerous carriers operate direct flights, including Alitalia (tel: 21 29 03 35 75, www.alitliausa.com), American Airlines (tel: 80 04 33 73 00, www.aa.com), Continental (tel: 80 02 31 08 56, www.continental.com), Delta (tel: 80 02 41 41 41, www.delta.com), Northwest Airlines (tel: 80 02 25 25 25, www.nwa.com) and United (tel: 80 05 38 29 29, www.ual.com). Flying time varies from around 11 hours (US west coast) to 8 hours (eastern US).

Ticket prices tend to be highest at Christmas, Easter and throughout the summer. Airport taxes are generally included in ticket prices.

By Rail Numerous fast and overnight services operate to Milan and Venice from most European capitals, with connections to Bergamo, Brescia and Verona. Motorail services are also available to Verona and Bolzano (from Hamburg for example), to Nice from Calais (leaving just a relatively short drive east to the lakes) and from Denderleeuw (Belgium) to Milan and Venice. See www.trenitalia.it for details.

TIME

Italy is one hour ahead of GMT in winter, one hour ahead of BST in summer, six hours ahead of New York and nine hours ahead of Los Angeles. Clocks go forward one hour in March and go back in October.

CURRENCY & FOREIGN EXCHANGE

Currency The currency in Italy is the euro (€). There are 1, 2, 5, 10, 20 and 50 cent coins and €1 and €2 coins. Notes are issued in denominations of €5, €10, €20, €50, €100, €200 and €500.

Exchange Most major travellers' cheques – the best way to carry money – can be changed at exchange kiosks *(cambio)* at the airports, at main railway stations and in exchange offices near major tourist sights. Many banks also have exchange desks but queues can be long.

Credit cards Most credit cards *(carta di credito* – but frequently the word tessera is used for 'card') are widely accepted in major hotels, restaurants and shops, but cash is often preferred in smaller establishments and generally everywhere in the more rural areas. Credit cards can also be used to obtain cash from ATM cash dispensers.

ITALIAN STATE TOURIST BOARD ➤ WWW.ENIT.IT

In the UK
1 Princes Street
London W1R 8AY
☎ 020 74 08 12 54

In the US
630 Fifth Avenue, Suite 1565
New York NY 10111
☎ 21 22 45 56 18

In Australia
Level 45, 1 Macquarie Street
Sydney NSW 2000
☎ 02 93 92 79 00

Practicalities

NATIONAL HOLIDAYS

1 January	*Capodanno* – New Year's Day
6 January	Epiphany
March/Apr	*Pasqua* – Easter
March/Apr	*Pasquetta* – Easter Monday
25 Apr	Liberation Day
1 May	*Festa del Lavoro* – Labour Day
24 June	*San Giovanni* – St John's Day
15 Aug	Assumption of the Virgin Mary
1 Nov	*Tutti Santi* – All Saints' Day
8 Dec	Immaculate Conception
25 Dec	*Natale* – Christmas Day
26 December	*Santo Stefano* – St Stephen's Day

ELECTRICITY

The current is 220 volts AC, 50 cycles. Plugs are of the round two-pin continental type; UK and North American visitors will require an adaptor. North American visitors should check whether 110/120-volt AC appliances require a voltage transformer.

OPENING HOURS

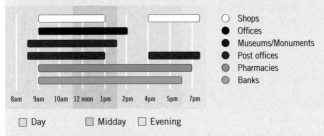

○ Shops
● Offices
● Museums/Monuments
● Post offices
● Pharmacies
● Banks

8am 9am 10am 12 noon 1pm 2pm 4pm 5pm 7pm

☐ Day   ☐ Midday   ☐ Evening

Shops Hours vary but they are usually open Mon–Sat 8–1, 4–8, Mon 4–8pm
Shops in larger cities open all day *(orario continuato)*
Restaurants 12.30–3, 6.30–10.30 pm.
Museums Hours vary greatly, most close on Mon
Banks Usually Mon–Fri 8.30–1.30
Post offices Mon–Fri 8:15–2, Sat 8:15–noon or 2

TIPS/GRATUITIES

Tipping rates in Italy are low. Restaurant, café and hotel bills include a service charge so a tip is not expected, although many people leave a few coins in restaurants and up to 10 percent in smart ones. **Taxis:** Round up to nearest €0.50; **Porters:** €0.50–€1 per bag; **Chambermaids:** €0.50–€1 per day; **Lavatory attendants:** Small change

TIME DIFFERENCES

Garda (CET)	London (GMT)	New York (EST)	Los Angeles (PST)	Sydney (AEST)
12 noon	← 11 noon	← 6am	← 3am	→ 9pm

STAYING IN TOUCH

Post Letter boxes are red for normal post and blue for priority post *(posta prioritaria)*. Stamps *(francobolli)* can be bought from post offices, tobacconists showing a 'T' sign and bars.

Public telephones Most payphones require a phone card *(carta telefonica)*, bought from post offices, shops or bars. Tear the corner off the card before use. There are hardly any coin-operated public phones left. The **area code** is an integral part of Italian telephone numbers. When ringing from abroad and for local calls the area code or prefix including the '0' must always be dialled as well. Dial 170 for the operator or 12 40 for directory enquiries.

International Dialling Codes:
Dial 00 followed by

UK	44
USA / Canada	1
Irish Republic	353
Australia	61
Italy	39

Mobile phones Mobile or cell phones *(telefono cellulare* or the more popular *telefonino)* automatically seek out an appropriate Italian partner network (roaming). The '0' is however not dialled (also applies to calls from abroad). The max. price specified by the EU applies to mobile phone calls. Anyone travelling around Italy for a longer period may find a prepaid chip from the Italian TIM better value. Skype provides cost-free telephoning both within Italy and abroad (www.skype.com).

WiFi and Internet Most hotels have a Wi-Fi connection (sometimes liable to charges) that can be accessed in all guest rooms and reception areas.

PERSONAL SAFETY

Petty crime, particularly the theft of wallets and handbags, is fairly common in major cities. Be aware of scruffy, innocent-looking children: they may be working in gangs, fleecing unwary tourists. If approached, hang on to your possessions, raise your voice and – if necessary – push them away. To be safe:

- Carry money in a belt or pouch.
- Hang your camera around your neck – never put it down.
- Leave valuables in the hotel safe.
- Stick to main, well-lit streets at night

Police assistance:
☎ 113 from any phone

	EMERGENCY	112
	POLICE	113
	FIRE	115
	AMBULANCE	118

Practicalities

HEALTH

 Insurance Nationals of EU countries can get medical treatment at a reduced cost in Italy with the relevant documentation (on presentation of an EHIC card for UK residents, contact the post office for latest regulations), although medical insurance is still advised and is essential for all other visitors.

 Dental Services As for general medical treatment, nationals of EU countries can obtain dental treatment at a reduced cost, but private medical insurance is still advised for all.

 Weather Minor health worries include too much sun, dehydration or mosquito bites, so drink plenty of fluids and wear sunscreen and a hat in summer. Insect repellent may be useful if you sleep with the windows open in summer.

 Drugs Prescription and other medicines are available from a pharmacy *(farmacia)*, indicated by a green cross. Pharmacies usually open at the same times as shops (Mon–Sat 8–1, 4–8), and take it in turns to stay open through the afternoon, late evenings and on Sundays.

 Safe Water Tap water is safe. So, too, is water from public drinking fountains unless marked *acqua non potabile*.

CONCESSIONS

Young People/Senior Citizens Young visitors and children under 18 from EU countries are entitled to free entrance or reduced rates to most galleries. Similar concessions are available to senior citizens over 65. A passport is required as proof of age.

Combined Entry Tickets If you are planning a lot of sight-seeing in one area, enquire at the tourist office or at participating sites about combined tickets which offer much better value than buying individual tickets. For example, in Vicenza, a combined entrance ticket is available for all the city's main attractions.

TRAVELLING WITH A DISABILITY

Wheelchair access is improving in larger cities but is almost non-existent in the rest of the country. In old towns, you'll find few pavements or dropped kerbs, streets can be narrow, cobbled and congested with parked vehicles.

In the UK Holiday Care (tel: 084 51 24 99 71, www.holidaycare.org.uk) publishes information on accessibility.

In the US SATH (Society for Accessible Travel and Hospitality, www.sath.org) has lots of tips for travellers with visual impairment or reduced mobility.

CHILDREN

Children are welcome in most hotels and restaurants. Many attractions offer reductions. Special attractions for kids are marked out with the logo shown above.

RESTROOMS

There are public lavatories (WC/restrooms) at railway stations, in larger museums and in bars for customers to use.

Ask for *il bagno* or *il gabinetto*.

EMBASSIES AND CONSULATES

UK (Rome)	USA (Rome)	Ireland (Rome)	Australia (Rome)	Canada (Rome)
☎ 06 42 20 00 01	☎ 06 46 74 1	☎ 06 5 85 23 81	☎ 06 85 27 21	☎ 06 85 44 41
www.gov.uk	italy.usembassy.gov	www.dfa.ie/irish-embassy/italy	www.italy.embassy.gov.au	Italy.gc.ca

Useful Words and Phrases

SURVIVAL PHRASES

yes/no **sì/non**
please **per favore**
Thank you **grazie**
You're welcome **di niente/prego**
I'm sorry **mi dispiace**
goodbye **arrivederci**
good morning **buongiorno**
goodnight **buona sera**
how are you? **come sta?**
how much? **quanto costa?**
I would like... **vorrei...**
open **aperto**
closed **chiuso**
today **oggi**
tomorrow **domani**
Monday **lunedì**
Tuesday **martedì**
Wednesday **mercoledì**
Thursday **giovedì**
Friday **venerdì**
Saturday **sabato**
Sunday **domenica**

DIRECTIONS

I'm lost **mi sono perso/a**
Where is...? **dove si trova...?**
  the station **la stazione**
  the telephone **il telefono**
  the bank **la banca**
  the toilet **il bagno**
Turn left **volti a sinistra**
Turn right **volti a destra**
Go straight on **Vada dritto**
At the corner **all'angolo**
the street **la strada**
the building **il palazzo**
the traffic light **il semaforo**
the crossroads **l'incrocio**
the signs for... **le indicazione per...**

IF YOU NEED HELP

Help! **Aiuto!**
Could you help me, please?
  Mi potrebbe aiutare?
do you speak English? **Parla inglese?**
I don't understand **Non capisco**
Please could you call a doctor quickly?
  **Mi chiami presto un medico,
  per favore**

RESTAURANT

I'd like to book a table
  Vorrei prenotare un tavolo
A table for two please
  Un tavolo per due, per favore
Could we see the menu, please?
  Ci porta la lista, per favore?
What's this? **Cosa è questo?**
A bottle of/a glass of...
  Un bottiglia di/un bicchiere di...
Could I have the bill?
  Ci porta il conto?

ACCOMMODATION

Do you have a single/double room?
  Ha una camera singola/doppia?
with/without bath/toilet/shower
  con/senza vasca/gabinetto/doccia
Does that include breakfast?
  E'inclusa la prima colazione?
Does that include dinner?
  E'inclusa la cena?
Do you have room service?
  C'è il servizio in camera?
Could I see the room?
  E' possibile vedere la camera?
I'll take this room **Prendo questa**
Thanks for your hospitality
  Grazie per l'ospitalità

NUMBERS

0 **zero**	12 **dodici**	40 **quaranta**	400 **quattrocento**
1 **uno**	13 **tredici**	50 **cinquanta**	500 **cinquecento**
2 **due**	14 **quattordici**	60 **sessanta**	600 **seicento**
3 **tre**	15 **quindici**	70 **settanta**	700 **settecento**
4 **quattro**	16 **sedici**	80 **ottanta**	800 **ottocento**
5 **cinque**	17 **diciassette**	90 **novanta**	900 **novecento**
6 **sei**	18 **diciotto**	100 **cento**	1,000 **mille**
7 **sette**	19 **diciannove**	101 **cento uno**	2,000 **duemila**
8 **otto**	20 **venti**	110 **centodieci**	10,000 **diecimila**
9 **nove**	21 **ventuno**	120 **centoventi**	
10 **dieci**	22 **ventidue**	200 **duecento**	
11 **undici**	30 **trenta**	300 **trecento**	

Useful Words and Phrases

acciuga anchovy
acqua water
affettati sliced cured meats
affumicato smoked
aglio garlic
agnello lamb
anatra duck
antipasti hors d'oeuvres
arista roast pork
arrosto roast
asparagi asparagus
birra beer
bistecca steak
bollito boiled meat
braciola minute steak
brasato braised
brodo broth
bruschetta toasted bread with garlic or tomato topping
budino pudding
burro butter
cacciagione game
cacciatore, alla rich tomato sauce with mushrooms
caffè corretto/macchiato coffee with liqueur/spirit, or with a drop of milk
caffè freddo iced coffee
caffè latte milky coffee
caffè lungo weak coffee
caffè ristretto strong coffee
calamaro squid
cappero caper
carciofo artichoke
carota carrot
carne meat
carpa carp
casalingo homemade
cassata Sicilian fruit ice cream
cavolfiore cauliflower
cavolo cabbage
ceci chickpeas
cervello brains
cervo venison
cetriolino gherkin
cetriolo cucumber
cicoria chicory
cinghiale boar
cioccolata chocolate
cipolla onion
coda di bue oxtail
coniglio rabbit

contorni vegetables
coperto cover charge
coscia leg of meat
cotolette cutlets
cozze mussels
crema custard
crostini canape with savoury toppings or croutons
crudo raw
digestivo after-dinner liqueur
dolci cakes/desserts
erbe aromatiche herbs
facito stuffed
fagioli beans
fagiolini green beans
faraona guinea fowl
fegato liver
finocchio fennel
formaggio cheese
forno, al baked
frittata omelette
fritto fried
frizzante fizzy
frulatto whisked
frutta fruit
frutti di mare seafood
funghi mushrooms
gamberetto shrimp
gelato ice cream
ghiaccio ice
gnocchi potato dumplings
granchio crab
gran(o)turco corn
griglia, alla grilled
imbottito stuffed
insalata salad
IVA VAT
latte milk
lepre hare
lumache snails
manzo beef
merluzzo cod
miele honey
minestra soup
molluschi shellfish
olio oil
oliva olive
ostrica oyster
pancetta bacon
pane bread
panino roll
panna cream
parmigiano Parmesan
passata sieved or creamed

pastasciutta dried pasta cooked, with sauce
pasta sfoglia puff pastry
patate fritte chips
pecora mutton
pecorino sheep's milk cheese
peperoncino chilli
peperone red/green pepper
pesce fish
petto breast
piccione pigeon
piselli peas
pollame fowl
pollo chicken
polpetta meatball
porto port wine
prezzemolo parsley
primo piatto first course
prosciutto cured ham
ragù meat sauce
ripieno stuffed
riso rice
salsa sauce
salsiccia sausage
saltimbocca veal with prosciutto and sage
secco dry
secondo piatto main course
senape mustard
servizio compreso service charge included
sogliola sole
spuntini snacks
succa di frutta fruit juice
sugo sauce
tonno tuna
uovo affrogato/in carnica poached egg
uovo al tegamo/fritto fried egg
uovo alla coque soft boiled egg
uovo alla sodo hard boiled egg
uova strapazzate scambled egg
verdure vegetables
vino bianco white wine
vino rosato rosé wine
vino rosso red wine
vitello veal
zucchero sugar
zucchino courgette
zuppa soup

Road Atlas

For chapters: see inside front cover

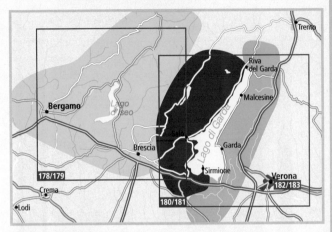

Key to Road Atlas

A14 2	Motorway
E 55	Dual carriageway
SS16	Trunk road
	Main road
	Secondary road
	Road under construction/development
	Tunnel
	Railroad
	Ferry
	International-, province boundary
	National park, National preserve
	Restricted area
★	TOP 10
26	Don't Miss
22	At Your Leisure

✈	International airport
✈	Regional airport
♱ ♰	Monastery / Church, chapel
♦ ♦	Castle, fortress / Ruin
★	Point of interest
∴	Archaeological site
Î Ï	Tower / Lighthouse
∭ ∩	Waterfall / Cave, grotto
▲)(	Mountain peak / Pass
Ⓐ 🕉	Campground / Lookout point
î ✚	Information / Hospital
M̂ 🎭	Museum / Theatre, opera house
✿ ✉	Police / Post office
⚓ 🏖	Harbour, mooring / (Swimming) beach
P P	Multi-storey / Parking

1 : 330 000

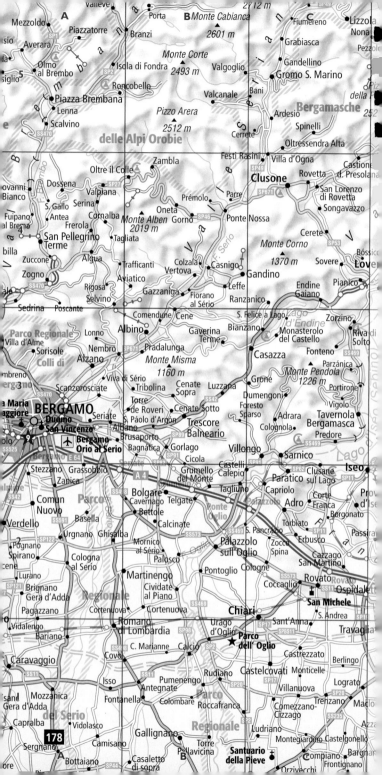

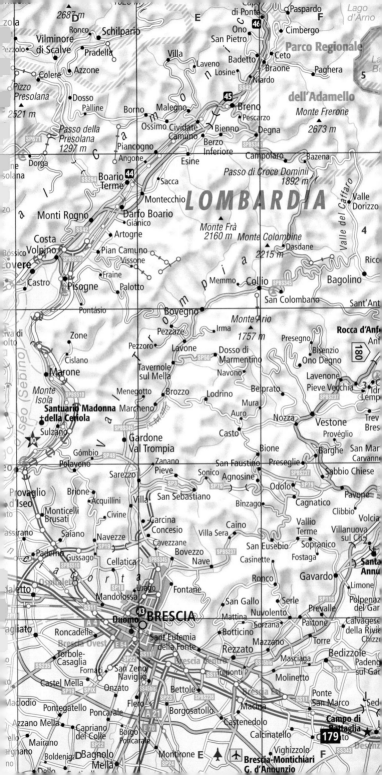

Bienno
Degna
2673 m
Creto
Strada
Monte Cadria
2254 m
erzo feriore
Campolaro
Bazena
Prezzo
Passo di Croce Dominii
1892 m
Castel Sondino
Grotta Rossa
2192 m
Brione
Cimego
Tiarno-di-Sotto
Tiarno-di-Sopra
Bezze
nte Frà
60 m
Monte Colombine
2215 m
Valle Dorizzo
Ca'Rossa
Storo
Condino
Lago di Ampolla
Val d'Ampola
Monte Tren
1974 m
Lago di Le

OMBARDIA
5
Memmo
Collio
SPBS345
Riccomassimo
Lodrone
SS237
SS240
Passo di Tremalzo
1694 m

a
Dasdane
San Colombano
Bagolino
Ponte Caffaro
Cima Spessa
1820 m
Parco Region

Irma
Monte Ario
1757 m
Presegno
Sant'Antonio
Bondone
Magasa
Cádria
dell' Alto
Tren

Dc4so di Marmentino
Navono
Blsenzio
Ono Degno
Rocca d'Anfo
18
Anfo
Vesta
Persone
Moerna
Piev
Campi del Ga
Tignale
14

odrino
Belprato
Mura
Auro
Lavenone
Pieve Vecchia
Crone
Idro
Lemprato
Vantone
Capovalle
Bresciano
Lago di Valvestino
Costa
Piovere Olde
Briano

Casto
179
Bione
Nozza
Vestone
Provéglio
Treviso
Bresciano
Eno
17
M. Zingla
1497 m
Gargnano
15
Castell di Brenz

San Faustino
Preseglie
Barghe
San Martino
Carvanno
M. Spino
1486 m
Rif. Pirlo
Valle Tocolano
Bogliaco
Gaino
16
Villa
VILLA BETTONI
Pai

Agnosine
P79
Odolo
SP79
Sabbio Chiese
Pavone
Sant'Urbano
Vobarno
Sanico
Maclino
Toscolano-
19
Maderno
Crero

3 Binzago
Caino
Sera
Cagnatico
Clibbio
Roe
Volciano
Villanuova sul Clisi
Vallio Terme
Sopranico
VILLA IL VITTORIALE
Gardone Riviera
Torri del Benaco
Acque Fredde
29
Monte Luppia
418 m

San Eusebio
Casinette
Fostaga
Ronco
Gavardo
SS45bis
Santa Maria Annunziata
Salò
Porto Portese
Isola del Garda
20
SR249

San Gallo
Serle
Limone
Pieve Vecchia
del Benaco
Polpenazze del Garda
Prevalle
SP116
SP572
Balbiana
Isola San Biagio
Punta Belvedere
Manerba del Garda
San Viglio
28
Punta San Vigilio
Garda
3

Mattina
Nuvolento
Sorzana
Paitone
Calvagese della Riviera
Chizzoline
SS25
Moniga del Garda
Bardolino
Cavaion Vero
Cisano
27

Botticino
Mazzano
Torre
Bedizzole
Padenghe sul Garda
Grotte di Catullo
Sirmione
Madonna delle Pergolana
Lazise
26

Rezzato
SS45bis
Masciaga
Molinetto
Lido di Lonato
Desenzano del Garda
Fossalta

Treponti
Macina
Castenedolo
Ponte San Marco
Sedena
Campo di Battaglia
Lonato
21
Rivoltella
SS11
Colombare
Lugana
Gardaland
25
Peschiera del Garda

Calcinatello
Vighizzolo
Calcinato
SS343
Desenzano
SS567
Le Tassere
SR11
Ponti sul Minico
SP10

Brescia-Montichiari
G. d'Annunzio
Ro
Montichiari
Esenta
Centenaro
A 4 70
22
Madonna del Frassino
SP13
24
Salionze

Case Oriani
Novagli
SPBS236
SPBS668
SS567
Castel Venzago
Abbazia di San Vigilio
San Martino della Battaglia
Pozzolengo
Monzamba

Malpaga
Calvisano
180
Mezzane
SS343
Castiglione delle Stiviere
Pozzo Catena
22
Solferino
Castellaro Lagusello
Parco Giardino Sigurtà
Borghetto

Carpenedolo
S. Vigilio
SS236
SP8
Cavriana
Campagnolo

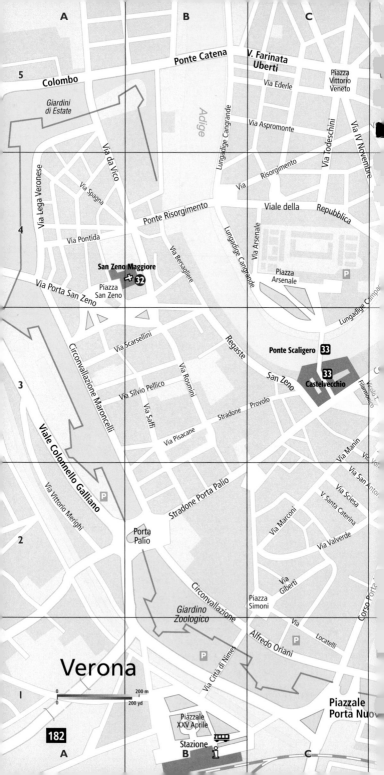

Verona

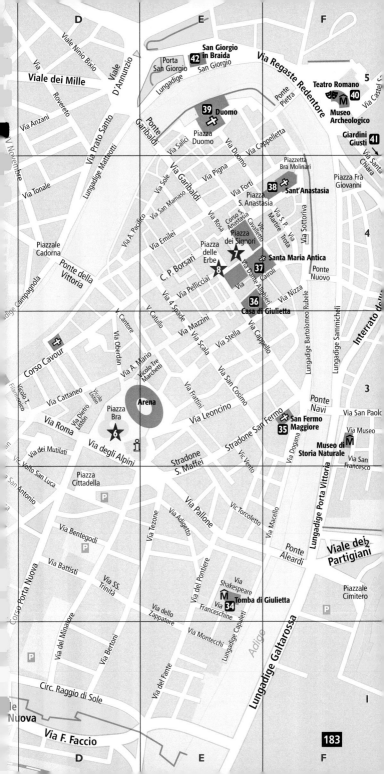

D   E   F

Viale Ninio Bixio

Via

Porta
San Giorgio

42 San Giorgio
in Braida
San Giorgio

Via Regaste Redentore

Viale dei Mille

Viale
D'Annunzio

Rovereto

Via Anzani

Via Prato Santo

Lungadige

Lungadige Matteotti

Ponte
Garibaldi

Lungadige

Ponte
Pietra

Via Castel S

39 Duomo

Teatro Romano
M **40**

5

Via Tonale

Piazza
Duomo

Via Salici

Via Duomo

Via Cappelletta

Museo
Archeologico

Piazzale
Cadorna

Via A. Pacifico

Via Garibaldi

Via Sole

Via San Mamaso

Via Pigna

Via Forti

Piazzetta
Bra Molinari

Giardini
Giusti **41**

Via Santa
Chiara

Piazza Frà
Giovanni

Ponte della
Vittoria

Via Emilei

Via Rosa

Via S. Anastasia

Corso S. Anastasia

38 Sant'Anastasia

Via S. P.
Martire

Piazza
S. Anastasia

Via Sottoriva

4

C. P. Borsari

Piazza
delle
Erbe

Piazza
dei Signori

7

Via Cavaletto

Via Trota

37 Santa Maria Antica

Ponte
Nuovo

Lungadige Campagnola

V. Cantore

Via Oberdan

V. Catullo

Via 4 Spade

Via Pellicciai

8

Via Dante

Via Cairoli

Via Dante Alighieri

Via Nizza

Lungadige Bartolomeo Rubele

Lungadige Sammicheli

Interrato de

36 Casa di Giulietta

Corso Cavour

Via Cattaneo

Via A. Mario

Vicolo Tre
Marchetti

Via Mazzini

Via Stella

Via Cappello

Vicolo F.
Filomoto

Via Dietro
Listón

Arena

Via Frattini

Via San Cosimo

Ponte
Navi

Via San Paolo

3

Via Roma

Piazza
Bra

6

Via Scala

Via Leoncino

Via Vento

Stradone San Fermo

San Fermo
Maggiore **35**

Via Museo
M

Via degli Alpini

Stradone
S. Maffei

Via Dogana

Museo di
Storia Naturale

Via San
Francesco

Via Vetro San Luca

Vic. Porta San Luca

Via San Antonio

Piazza
Cittadella

P

Via Pallone

Vic Torcoletto

Via Macello

Ponte
Aleardi

Lungadige Porta Vittoria

Viale dei
Partigiani

2

Via Bentegodi

P

Via Tezone

Via Adigetto

Piazzale
Cimitero

Via Battisti

Via SS
Trinità

Via del Pontiere

Via
Shakespeare

M

Tomba di Giulietta

P

P

Via dello
Zappatore

Via
Franceschine

34

Via Capuleti

Via Montecchi

Lungadige Capuleti

Adige

Lungadige Galtarossa

P

Via del Minatore

Via Bertoni

Via del Fante

le
Nuova

Circ. Raggio di Sole

I

Via F. Faccio

D   E   F

Index

Index

Index

Index

Picture Credits

Credits

1st Edition 2016

Worldwide Distribution: Marco Polo Travel Publishing Ltd
Pinewood, Chineham Business Park
Crockford Lane, Chineham
Basingstoke, Hampshire RG24 8AL, United Kingdom.
© MAIRDUMONT GmbH & Co. KG, Ostfildern

Authors: Richard Sale, Frances Wolverton, Jochen Müssig
Editor: Robert Fischer (www.vrb-muenchen.de)
Revised editing and translation: Christopher Wynne
Program supervisor: Birgit Borowski
Chief editor: Rainer Eisenschmid

Cartography: © MAIRDUMONT GmbH & Co. KG, Ostfildern
3D-illustrations: jangled nerves, Stuttgart

Printed in China

Despite all of our authors' thorough research, errors can creep in.
The publishers do not accept any liability for this. Whether you
want to praise, alert us to errors or give us a personal tip –
please don't hesitate to email or post:

MARCO POLO Travel Publishing Ltd
Pinewood, Chineham Business Park
Crockford Lane, Chineham
Basingstoke, Hampshire RG24 8AL
United Kingdom
Email: sales@marcopolouk.com

FSC
www.fsc.org
MIX
Paper from
responsible sources
FSC® C124385

10 REASONS
TO COME BACK AGAIN

1. Compared to the rest of Italy Lake Garda is relatively **cheap**. You get a lot for a little.

2. The **mountains and water** complement each other beautifully especially in the north.

3. You can't get enough of the **changing light** on the lake that ranges from black to golden.

4. One **trip around the lake** is definitively not enough!

5. Each of the **five islands** begs to be visited – by wading, on an airbed or by boat.

6. The *lago* is Europe's best freshwater playground for **surfers**. If that's not reason enough …

7. **Aperol** and 'Hugo' don't taste nearly as good at home.

8. Not only the **Pizza World Champion** Giuseppe Conte in Bardolino bakes a perfect pizza.

9. New **spa hotels** can now keep you cosily warm in the low season too.

10. **Winter** on the lake can be beautiful – the peace and quiet is as if the lake were on holiday too…